SILVER JUBILEE

Bognor Regis Local History Society

Celebrating

25 YEAR S

1979 - 2004

A
SELECTION
of

NEWSLETTER ARTICLES

written by

RON IDEN

(Re-printed in this special edition)

Published by
The Bognor Regis Local History Society

October 2004

ISBN 0 950 74558 8

Printed in Great Britain by
Mulberry Press, Bognor Regis
West Sussex

FOREWORD

RON IDEN – A LOCAL HISTORIAN

I wrote a letter to The Bognor Post in October 1973 in support of the then rather beleaguered campaign to save Hotham Park House. The Chairman of the Friends of Hotham Park House, Mrs Jean Barry Rose, read my letter in the paper and, on the strength of my apparent concern and youth, invited me to join the Committee. "There is one other young person on the Committee," she encouraged me. "He is called Mr Iden and he is a postman." She went on to assure me that I would like him. She was right.

I certainly liked Ron. He is eminently likeable. He was also a kindred spirit on a Committee devoted less to historical research than cheese and wine parties and writing occasional letters to the Press. He was also young and had a genuine enthusiasm for the history of Bognor, a town which he believed had by then been systematically abused by the concrete and car park brutalism of the 1960s.

In an age in which conservation and environmental awareness are now mainstream, it is hard to remember the post war apathy and sometimes open hostility to local historical heritage. The late Gerard Young had been, throughout the 1960s, a lone and sometimes desperate voice in the wilderness, as layer upon layer of Bognor's Georgian and Victorian inheritance had been swept aside in the so-called pursuit of progress. It is sometimes forgotten that Ron Iden was as a boy a friend, if not a protégé, of Gerard Young, who had actively encouraged Ron to build up and conserve a personal archive of historical material, and, above all, to photograph a rapidly vanishing landscape of Bognor's past.

However, to compare these two men would be unfair. Young was a journalist, a campaigner and populist historian using, and sometimes embellishing, the past to make sound conservationist points. Ron Iden was, and always has been, a cautious and careful archivist and scholar. His perfectionism has made him a special kind of local historian, as is evidenced by his collected writings.

The threat to Hotham Park House was, as it happened, the high water mark of philistinism towards Bognor's past. The late Councillor Leslie Walwin, a powerful Bognor politician in his day, had commented angrily in 1974 (largely to annoy the fledgeling conservation movement), that Billy Butlin had done more for Bognor than Sir Richard Hotham, whilst Walwin's political lieutenant, Councillor Jimmy Shearing, boasted to the Bognor Post that he looked forward to driving into Hotham Park House on a bulldozer.

We were both young and very angry. I persuaded Ron that his obvious skills as a writer and historian should lead him to write an account of the historical and architectural worth of Hotham Park House. Ron was characteristically diffident and modest, and it took some time to persuade him. However, with some encouragement we produced a simple booklet and circulated it widely. Hotham Park House was, entirely by chance, saved by a sympathetic developer, perhaps an indication in itself of changing fashion.

Another, more tangible, indication was the foundation of the Bognor Regis Local History Society in 1979. The story of this foundation has been often told, with much credit being given to the late Kenneth Richmond Crum whose idea it was, or to myself who served as the Society's first Chairman. The truth is that Ron's influence on the Society at its inception was greater by far than Ken's or mine. It was Ron who drew together the list of local history enthusiasts to that first meeting and who guided Kenneth Crum's initial ideas. Indeed, that first meeting was remarkable in that Ron made a speech – I suspect the only public pronouncement he has ever made. Such is his modesty and self deprecation that he described his oratory on that occasion as more of a squeak than a speech.

More importantly, local enthusiasts have come and gone, but Ron has been a constant guiding hand in the Society's development over the last twenty five years, acting not only as Editor of the newsletter, but as the conscience of the Society. He has always been anxious that accuracy and sound research should underpin any project. Ron has encouraged, advised and punctiliously edited countless research projects undertaken by aspiring and established local historians, often acting as a bridge between such historians both outside and within the Society, encouraging the sharing of information.

Ron Iden has forgotten more about Bognor's history than anyone else knows and his meticulous dogged research into the life of Sir Richard Hotham is an object lesson in perseverance and accuracy. This book brings together a variety of themes and topics written over the years by Ron Iden. Their common thread is his scholarship and high standards.

David Allam

(First Chairman)

CONTENTS

Bricks and Mortar

The Three Rs and more

"Commerce"

INTRODUCTION

The Bognor Regis Local History Society was conceived in January 1979 when twenty three "persons interested in local history" met in the Public Library to discuss their interest in the preservation of the town's heritage. During the ensuing twenty five years the Society has created a collection of local artefacts, photographs and documents, and a Museum in which to display some of them for the benefit of both local people and visitors to the town. It has organized lectures on local and historical topics, arranged walks and visits to places of interest, and encouraged researchers to pursue their own historical projects. Some of that research has culminated in the production of books for sale to the public, many of which are bought by historians from outside the locality to aid their own investigations. Other items have appeared as articles in the twice-yearly Newsletters.

Chief among the researchers has been Ron Iden, one of the founder members who instigated that inaugural meeting in 1979, and for many of the last twenty five years the Editor of the Newsletter. It seems appropriate to celebrate the Society's Silver Jubilee by producing a collection of some of his articles, which together make an interesting account of the town's history, and which we feel will be an enjoyable introduction for newcomers to Bognor Regis, and a welcome addition to the bookshelves of members of the Society and others with an interest in our heritage.

In addition this special anniversary is an opportunity to thank all those who over the past twenty five years have contributed to the running of the Society and its Museum, as well as those who have enriched our lives by arranging or giving lectures, or exhibiting or publishing the results of their own meticulous research. Much has been done to raise the town's awareness of its heritage, and to record and preserve it for posterity. We trust this publication will play its part as we look forward to the next twenty five years.

Jane Barnes

(Present Chairman)

ABOUT THE AUTHOR

Ron Iden was born into a Bognor family after World War II. He declines to reveal the exact date. He has lived in the area all his life and was educated at South Bersted C of E Primary School and William Fletcher School (now the Community College), and studied history as a mature student at the West Sussex Institute of Higher Education (now part of University College, Chichester). Since 1987 he has worked in the searchroom at the West Sussex Records Office, where he has provided valuable assistance to innumerable researchers and authors. His name is frequently to be found among the acknowledgements in publications on local history. He is a co-founder of Bognor Regis Local History Society, and has been closely associated with its newsletter, either as editor or chief contributer, since its inception twenty five years ago. Bognor Regis Local History Society is proud to present a selection of the articles Ron has produced over those twenty five years.

Sir Richard

WHO WAS SIR RICHARD HOTHAM?

(Newsletter no 16, February 1987, updated 2004)

Born 5th October 1722, son of Joseph and Sarah Hotham, who are buried at Skelton Church, 3 miles north of York.

Baptised 9th November 1722 at Holy Trinity, King's Court, York.

Married 3rd December 1743 by special licence at Chelsea College Chapel.
(Richard Hotham, of St Giles in the Fields, Mdsx. 21+)
(Frances Atkinson, of Stockton on Tees, Durham. 25+)

Made two fortunes, as a hatter & hosier in London (initially in Searle St, Lincolns Inn) and in charter company dealings with the East India Company (ship's husband of four vessels).

He had a son, John, who died in infancy in 1751, and Frances, his first wife, died in 1760. On 7 April 1761 he married at St Martin-in-the-Fields, London, Barbara Huddart, who died 1 February 1777 aged 44.

Knighted 12th April 1769 for presenting a loyal address to King George III on behalf of the people of Surrey.

Created Sheriff of Surrey in 1770.

Author of two pamphlets, "Reflections on East India Shipping" (1773) and "A Candid State of Affairs relative to East India Shipping" (1774) attacking the East India Co's bad management.

In 1778 elected Chairman of Wimbledon Vestry Sub-Committee. Local Magistrate. Lived at Merton Place, (later Lord Nelson's home), and in 1792 built a smaller house, Merton Grove (Wimbledon Grove in his will).

In September 1780 elected MP for Southwark, defeating Dr Johnson's friend, Henry Thrale. Member of Whig opposition and follower of Charles James Fox.

After defeat in the July 1784 election, he first visited Bognor that summer (possibly on the suggestion of his charter company partner, Lieut Nathaniel Turner, who is thought to be a relative-by-marriage of the Rev Thomas Durnford, South Bersted's vicar).

Died 13 March 1799 and buried in South Bersted Churchyard.

An energetic, enthusiastic and ambitious social climber with an apparent desire to improve the state of things.

Sir Richard Hotham 1722 - 1799

THE TWO WIVES – AND ONE SON - OF SIR RICHARD HOTHAM

Recent exciting discoveries in London
concerning the founder of Bognor
(Newsletter no 45, August 2001)

On Friday 7 February 1777 the London newspaper 'The Morning Post and Daily Advertiser' carried the following notice:

'On Saturday last died at Brompton, Lady Hotham, wife of Sir Richard Hotham, of Merton Place, Surrey.'

Similar brief reports appeared in other London newspapers and in the 'Gentleman's Magazine' and 'Annual Register'.

Richard Hotham of the parish of St Giles, Westminster (he was born in York), had married Frances Atkinson of Stockton-on-Tees at Chelsea Hospital Chapel on 1 December 1743. He was then 21 years of age, she was '25+'. At the time of his wife's death in 1777, Sir Richard (knighted in 1769) was seven years away from setting foot in Bognor. He had a house and business in London, and a country home at Merton Place, with grounds that straddled the parish boundary between Merton and fashionable Wimbledon, where he involved himself in vestry affairs.

Subsequent biographers of the founder of modern Bognor, including Gerard Young in the 1960s, my own contribution to the 'Dictionary of National Biography: Missing Persons' (1993), and the latest Bognor Regis Heritage Project website entry, have stated that 'Lady Frances Hotham' died in 1777.

Mr Charles Butler, a founder member of this Society who died four years ago, was an indefatigable researcher into Bognor's past. In my obituary to him in Newsletter no 38, I recalled his special fascination with Hotham's pre-Bognor life – and his unremitting quest to discover the burial place of Frances Hotham. The wife of a knight, he reasoned, must surely be recorded on a memorial somewhere. So he wrote to libraries, Record Offices, and clergy around the country, even to readers of

'Country Life' in March 1978. Some Record Offices insist on a personal visit, and while in Yorkshire last year, I checked all the Brompton parishes.

Unbeknown to us, however, Frances had died 17 years earlier.

A year ago I was scanning the International Genealogical Index (IGI) for London. For those as yet uninitiated in the national obsession for tracing family history, the IGI is a surname index to baptisms and marriages extracted by the Mormons in Salt Lake City from (mostly C of E) parish registers, county by county. There are errors and omissions, but it is an invaluable index, and under 'Hotham' appeared an entry for John, son of a Richard and Frances, christened in the parish of St Martin-in-the-Fields, Westminster, on 12 June 1751. (Rate and poll books indicate that Hotham's business as Hatter & Hosier moved from Searle Street, Lincolns Inn, to the corner of Hungerford Market and The Strand, near Charing Cross, around 1750).

This was a revelation! By all previous accounts, Hotham's marriage was childless and no offspring are mentioned in his will. The parish registers held at Westminster City Archives, confirmed the entry: born 11 June 1751, baptized 12 June. Under 13 June, however, both the burial accounts book and the Sexton's Day Book record the burial fees for a John Hotham, no age given but 'C' for child, address: 'Strand'. It would appear then that the infant survived only a day or so, although curiously, I have yet to find his name in the burial registers proper, either for St Martin-in-the-Fields or for neighbouring parishes.

Out of curiosity, I checked the St Martin's burial register for Frances in 1777. On the 8 February was recorded Lady Barbara Hotham. The Sexton's Day Book confirmed her age as 44. I looked again at the IGI, and turned to the St Martin's marriage register. On 7 April 1761, Richard Hotham "of this Parish', and Barbara Huddart of the parish of St Margaret, Westminster, were married by licence, witnessed by Joseph and Patience Huddart. Barbara was the daughter of Joseph Huddart and Patience, née Rash, and was christened in 1733 in St Martin-in-the-Fields parish, where her father was described as a pawnbroker in 1750 (1); but a Joseph and a Patience who featured among at least eight siblings of Barbara on the IGI may have been the witnesses in 1761.

Barbara also had a cousin, yet another Joseph Huddart (1741 – 1816), born in Cumberland and recorded in the 'Dictionary of National Biography' as hydrographer and manufacturer. The DNB entry records:

"In 1771 he went to London on a visit to a brother of his father, described as a wealthy tradesman in Westminster, whose daughters had married Sir

Richard Hotham and Mr Dingwall, both shipowners and holders of East India stock. On the introduction of these persons he entered the service of the East India Company, and in 1778 was appointed commander of the ship Royal Admiral, in which he made four voyages to the East."

The Royal Admiral was one of several vessels owned by Sir Richard Hotham, and was the subject of a lawsuit in 1787 (2).

A further curiosity in Hotham's 1761 marriage entry was that the officiating minister was not the Vicar of St Martin's but the Rev John Hotham, Vicar of Aston Abbots, Bucks. Among his many other appointments was Chaplain-in-ordinary to George III in 1760, Prebendary of St Paul's 1763 – 1780, Bishop of Ossory 1779 – 82 and Bishop of Clogher 1782 – 1795. In early 1794 he succeeded his brother Charles as 9th Baronet. It is known that Sir Richard Hotham long sought association with the Hotham baronetcy to whom he was unrelated, and later adopted (unofficially) a variation of their coat of arms.

But the picture was not complete without finally tracing the death of Frances – now confirmed as Richard's first wife – sometime between her son's birth in 1751 and Hotham's remarriage in 1761. St Martin-in-the-Fields had proved a fruitful source so far, so it was back to the burial register. Two to four burials a day were recorded (1000 per year? Where on earth, or rather under the earth, did they put them all?) I finally found Frances Hotham, buried 14 August 1760, eight months before Hotham's remarriage. No age recorded, but 'W' for adult woman, and the burial account book confirmed 'Church Vt' [vault], £6.14s.6d, address; 'Strand'.

Hotham was knighted in 1769, so it was Barbara who assumed the title of 'Lady Hotham'; Frances had remained Mrs Hotham. If only Mr Butler knew that his 20 year old mystery is now solved!

But new discoveries produce fresh 'loose ends'. Lindsay Fleming's impressive 3-volume 'History of Pagham in Sussex' (1949) includes the development of Bognor, because Bognor and Bersted were once part of Pagham. Volume 2 (p548) contains undated portraits of Sir Richard Hotham and his wife (below). But which wife is pictured here? Is Mr Hotham under or over 38 years of age?

Who was the original artist? Fleming's list of Volume2 illustrations says merely: 'from miniatures by P.B., formerly in the possession of Richard S White, friend of Sir Richard'. Charles Butler in 1977 sought the advice of the National Portrait Gallery. Referring to Daphne Foskett's 'Dictionary of Miniature Painters', the gallery hazarded a guess at: 'Peter Brown (flourished 1766-91) who signed PB and, perhaps less likely, a P Brooke or Brookes, fl. 1740-49, of whose work there is an example in the Victoria and Albert Museum.....Brown is perhaps more likely on date.' And on date, in the portrait, Hotham's age would appear to be closer to 44 (in 1766) than 27 (in 1749), so Barbara is more likely as the wife in the miniature.

SIR RICHARD HOTHAM AND HIS WIFE

The caption to Fleming's illustration, 'Sir Richard Hotham, 1722-1799 and his wife', was probably added by Emery Walker Ltd, who engraved several portraits and maps for the author.

Where are those miniatures now? When Lindsay Fleming used them to illustrate a short article about Hotham in 'Scouting and Guiding, the Annual Review of the Bognor Regis and District Girl Guides and Boy Scouts' (1932) (3), he said they were 'now in a local collection' – perhaps his own? Or that of his father, James, who died in 1932, (Lindsay Fleming died in 1966)?

Finally, another 'loose end'.. Notes in the Gerard Young Collection (West Sussex Record Office), record that at the time of Hotham's election as MP for Southwark (1780-84, just before his first appearance in Bognor), his address was stated as Fludyer Street, off King Street, Westminster. (King Street ran parallel with Parliament Street; and Fludyer Street, previously Axe Yard, was a turning immediately south of Downing Street – it is now built over). London directories list him there as a merchant, in 1784; but in 1783 they *also* list a <u>John</u> Hotham, merchant, at the same address. It could have been a misprint, but calls for further investigation.

1 Westminster City Archives, 15/116.
2 Gerard Young, A History of Bognor Regis (1983), p5.
3 Worthing Reference Library, Local Studies section: Sussex Topographical Pamphlets, vol XXXV, item 5.
    I am grateful to the staff of Westminster City Archives and of Worthing Reference Library for their help.

NB The present splendid church of St Martin-in-the-Fields (the fourth to occupy the site) was completed in 1726, so this is the building in which Hotham married Barbara Hoddart in 1761. Its churchyard lay north of what is now Trafalgar Square. Further digging of fresh graves in the vaults beneath the church was prohibited in 1773, and the vaults were cleared in the 19th century.

THE TWO WIVES OF SIR RICHARD HOTHAM
(Newsletter no 46, March 2002)

Since this article appeared in the last Newsletter, I have obtained a copy of Sir Richard's will (all 19 pages). This identifies 'Richard S White, friend of Sir Richard' – former possessor of the miniature portraits of Hotham and his wife – as Richard Samuel White, Hotham's lawyer of Lincoln's Inn in London, who drew up the original will.

....

SIR RICHARD HOTHAM'S ESTATE AT WIMBLEDON
(Newsletter no 46, March 2002)

When he died at Bognor in 1799, Sir Richard Hotham still owned and occasionally visited the Surrey home he had purchased while making his fortune in London. Wimbledon vestry minutes confirm that Sir Richard involved himself in parish affairs there in the 1770s, but confusion has reigned long over exactly which house (or houses) Hotham built or owned there, and when.

Various written sources were contradictory on whether Hotham actually built Merton Place (later owned by Lord Nelson), or alternatively, the less grandiose house – named as Merton Grove or 'Hotham House' near the double turnpike gates to the west of Merton Place. Gerard Young's 'History of Bognor Regis' is definite about Merton Grove, but less so concerning the 'slight' evidence that Hotham 'may' have built Nelson's mansion (1). And even the Victoria County History of Surrey (vol IV, 1911) confused Merton Place with another of the same name, built opposite Merton parish church, in the early 18th century. In documents of 1775 and 1791 (2) Hotham himself identified his home as Merton Place, but correspondence of 1796-97, concerning his dispute over the licensing of his Bognor chapel (3) – and his 1797 will (4) – refer to 'Wimbledon Grove'.

To a non-local, the puzzle was not made easier by the fact that the parish boundary running east-west along the Tooting to Morden turnpike road (now Merton High Street), consigned Nelson's Merton Place to Merton, while most of its grounds lay in Wimbledon to the north; Merton *Grove*, meanwhile, was all in Wimbledon.

But now we have a clearer picture. Hotham *rebuilt* one house, sold it and built the other. Richard Milward, Wimbledon local historian and author, clarified the matter with me when he was seeking a portrait of Hotham for his 'Wimbledon Two Hundred Years Ago' published in 1996; but still the fine detail, and his sources, remained hazy. In 1998, however, Merton Historical Society published 'A History of Lord Nelson's Merton Place', the result of research by Peter Hopkins, principally at the Minet Library, SE5, and among papers of the late John Wallace, local historian of Merton. Within the booklet's 47 pages are the details of Hotham's transactions, with dates, maps and above all – source references!

Merton Place, north and east fronts, 1805
(By courtesy of Merton Libraries & Heritage Services)

Merton Place, of Lord Nelson fame, was originally Moat House Farm, or Moat Farm, built in the early 1750s by Henry Pratt. His son, also Henry, sold it in November 1764 to 'Richard Hotham of St Martin in the Fields, merchant' (5). (A family connection is possible here, for as Mr Hopkins has noted, Hotham left in his will a £20 annuity to an "Eleanor Pratt of Roundcourt, Strand, a distant relative of mine").

Henry Pratt's 1753 insurance certificate referred to the house as 'Two storey and garrets, 46ft x 22 ft'. By 1792 when Hotham sold the property, it had been 'greatly enlarged and improved' but details of Hotham's alterations are not known. It has been said that certain features of the mansion which emerged – Merton Place – were replicated in the façade of Hotham Park House at Bognor. This idea is based, however, on the east front at Merton as depicted left of the centre tree in the 1805 view (above) *shortly after* the south wing had been extended in line with the north wing. This was, therefore, not the east front that Hotham knew. Gerard Young's suggestion that the *north* face of Merton Place may have influenced the design of *Dome House* in Bognor (1) makes more sense.

Along with the house, Hotham acquired in 1764 over 75 acres of land, 1½ of which surrounded the house, south of the turnpike road, in Merton; the rest lay north of the road in South Wimbledon. In 1769 he bought 7 more acres to the north-east, from Henry Thrale Esq of St Saviour's, Southwark (the same Henry Thrale whom Hotham successfully opposed in the Southwark election in 1780). And in February 1784 (months before he first visited Bognor), he linked these two pieces with the purchase of 44 acres from William Knight Welch and others, (see plan, below).

But in 1792, when his seaside resort in Sussex was well under way, Sir Richard sold the house and some 130 acres to Charles Greaves, William Hodgson, James Newton & John Leach, calico printers of Cheapside, London. They defaulted on a £10,000 debt in October 1793, but Charles Greaves repaid half and was allowed to keep the house, provided part of the estate was sold on his death, which occurred in 1800. In September 1801, the house and grounds (now reduced to a little over 50 acres) were acquired by Lord Nelson. He in turn expanded this again to over 160 acres with the purchase of a large adjoining estate to the west and to the south as far as Mitcham. Subsequent events are chronicled by Mr Hopkins; by 1823, the house had gone.

On selling his Wimbledon estate in 1792, Hotham had retained one field west of the crossroads opposite the present South Wimbledon Tube Station. On this he built a smaller house for himself, which he named Wimbledon Grove, later Merton Grove, which Gerard Young described in his 'History of Bognor Regis'. On Hotham's death in 1799, Merton Grove passed to another Wimbledon resident,

Merton Grove, drawn by John Hassell, c.1825

'Hotham House' by H P Burke, 1897
An illustration in 'Nelson and his Times', by Lord Charles Beresford and H W Wilson (Harmsworth Bros, 1897) – supposedly another view of Merton Grove but, oddly, bearing little resemblance to the house depicted above.

Benjamin Hays, who sold it in 1806 to Sir James Allan Park, a distinguished Judge who played a prominent part in parish affairs until his death in 1838. Hotham's house survived until the late 1890s but his name lives on in 'Hotham Road' which runs north from Merton High Street.

.Richard Hotham, too, was active at Wimbledon. On 12 April 1769, he and Timothy Waldo of Clapham presented the King with a loyal address disassociating the people of Surrey from the radical political agitations of John Wilkes. Both were rewarded with knighthoods and, a year later, *Sir* Richard became Sheriff of Surrey.

As related by Gerard Young, Hotham spent 3 years persuading both Wimbledon and Wandsworth Vestry Committees to maintain, as a public highway to Wandsworth, a drove-lane which ran through his land. Mr Young's assertion, that Hotham was then elected Vestry Chairman in 1778, has been refuted by Richard Milward of Wimbledon, who maintains he was Chairman only of a sub-committee, formed to look into the running of the workhouse. Nevertheless, Hotham's irrepressible desire to improve things led him a few years later to play a leading role in fund-raising and in organizing the repair and somewhat costly enlargement of Wimbledon parish church, reopened in 1788.

Somewhere beneath the tarmac in Bognor lie pieces of Wimbledon. William Bartlett's 'The History & Antiquities of the Parish of Wimbledon (1865) says of Hotham:
> 'He had so high an opinion of the gravel dug upon Wimbledon Common, that, at his expense, a large quantity was shipped in barges at Wandsworth to form the roads and paths of Bognor. There are still existing near that place, narrow paths between [hawthorn] hedges similar to the one called 'The Quicks', or the Quicksets, which was near Sir Richard Hotham's grounds at Wimbledon.'

Hotham's Spencer Terrace in Upper Bognor Road was named after one of his Wimbledon neighbours. The Spencers inherited the Manor of Wimbledon from Sarah Duchess of Marlborough in 1744. Her great-grandson John Spencer, created 1st Earl Spencer in 1765, spent more money on the Wimbledon estate than on the family seat at Althorp. (He was married to Georgiana Poyntz, whose two nephews were drowned in a boating accident off Aldwick in July 1815). His son, George John, was born at Wimbledon Park House in 1758 and became 2nd Earl in 1783, only to lose the house in a disastrous fire two years later. How well Hotham knew them personally (if at all) is not known, and deserves further research, but a 1776 plan of Wimbledon names no less than 'thirty Lords, Gentlemen and Esquires' as inhabitants. It was home to 13 MPs and 10 Cabinet Ministers between 1760 and

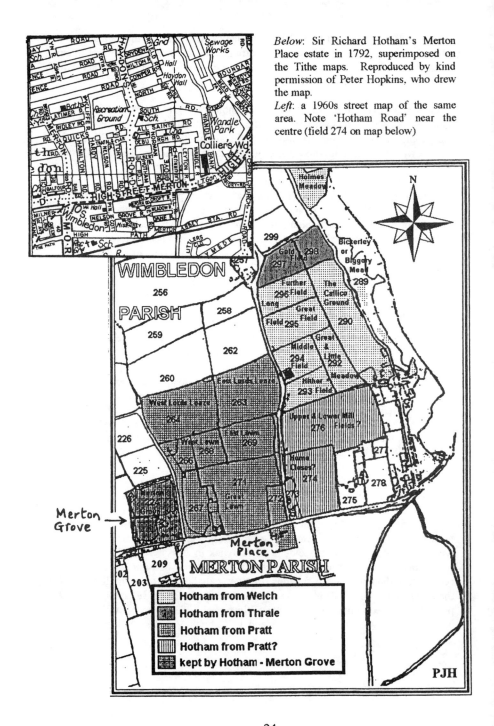

Below: Sir Richard Hotham's Merton Place estate in 1792, superimposed on the Tithe maps. Reproduced by kind permission of Peter Hopkins, who drew the map.

Left: a 1960s street map of the same area. Note 'Hotham Road' near the centre (field 274 on map below)

Merton Grove →

Hotham from Welch
Hotham from Thrale
Hotham from Pratt
Hotham from Pratt?
kept by Hotham - Merton Grove

PJH

1830, among them William Wilberforce and the Prime Minister, Lord Rockingham(6).

The reasons why Hotham, the social climber, settled in Wimbledon, are clearer than those that initially drew him to a sparsely populated stretch of Sussex shore. His activities at Merton Place, though, were something of a rehearsal for Bognor, where again he bought an old farmhouse, rebuilt it as a mansion (Bognor Lodge) and acquired land enough to build his seaside resort to attract the aristocracy whose patronage he craved. He could so easily have used land he already owned in already-fashionable Wimbledon. Instead, he created something unique at Bognor, and thereby saved it from becoming 'just an anonymous muddle on the coast' (7). The pity is that we have since destroyed so much of Sir Richard Hotham's legacy.

Sources
1. Gerard Young, *A History of Bognor Regis* (Phillimore, 1983), p42.
2. Sir Richard Hotham, *A Candid State of Affairs relative to East India Shipping* (2nd ed.1775); Memorial erected 1791 to his parents in Skelton parish church near York (see *Bognor Regis Post*, 18 January 1969).
3. Lambeth Palace Library, Moore Papers 4. See Ron Iden, 'Sir Richard Hotham's chapel at Bognor' in *Sussex Archaeological Collections*, vol 134 (1996), pp 179-183.
4. Public Record Office, PCC/PROB 11 1322, folio 271.
5. Lambeth Archives Department, Minet Library Deed 3764.
6. Richard Milward MA, *Wimbledon Two Hundred Years Ago* (The Milward Press, Coombe Lane, London SW20, 1996) pp 9,29,37.
    See also Charles Spencer, *The Spencer Family* (Viking [Penguin Group] 1999) esp pp 174-181 for the Wimbledon interlude.
7. Gerard Young's Column, *Bognor Regis Post*, 14 January 1967.

A History of Lord Nelson's Merton Place, published by Merton Historical Society, 1998, contains much more detail about the land transactions. It is available from Peter Hopkins, Publications Secretary, 57 Templecombe Way, Morden, Surrey, SM4 4JF, for £2.00 + 50p P&P. Cheques should be made payable to Merton Historical Society.

Notes on Old Bognor

BOGNOR'S COATS OF ARMS
or
A Tale of Pomp and Circumstances

(Newsletter No.8, January 1983)

Collectors of crested china will be familiar with Bognor's first town crest, which was adopted soon after the Urban District Council replaced the old Local Board in 1894. It's designer remains a mystery, but the 'Bognor Observer' featured it in the centre of it's masthead each week from August 1897 until June 1907. The design was a simple one - a shield divided vertically ('party per pale' in heraldic terms). with the Cornish Chough and gold and azure horizontal bars from the arms of Sir Richard Hotham, the town's founder, on the left hand side , and six traditional Sussex martlets on the other side. Hotham himself had unofficially adopted the arms of the naval family of the same name (to whom he was unrelated) substituting gold bars for the silver ones. A replica of them in stone may be seen on the front of Dome House, the central building of Sir Richard's Hothamton Crescent.

In 1934, the Council was rebuked by the Home Office, who had just woken up to the fact that the Council had been using the representation of the Crown in its Common Seal since the days of the Local Board. A year later, the town received a further blow to its pride when the Privy Council rejected an application for Borough status, on the grounds that Bognor's population fell some 2,000 short of the required 20,000; but the wound was partly healed by the granting by the College of Arms of an official coat of arms. "In outward formality, at any rate, the Council should soon be the very model of what a Council should be", commented the 'Bognor Regis Post' acidly

The new coat of arms was the handiwork of Councillor Commander Charles Edward Hudson, O.B.E., of Limmer Lane, Felpham. His blazoning dispensed with the Hotham features, but retained three of the Sussex martlets. The invected chief was said to represent the sea wall; the gold pile, the sands, the blue field and gull's wings, the town's association with the sea; and the crown, its association with King George V six years earlier. Also included was the motto 'Action' which represented more than met the eye.

Bognor Regis Local History Society

Hotham
baronetcy cr. 1622

Town Crest
c.1897

Sir Richard Hotham
Dome House, Bognor, c.1790.

BOGNOR REGIS

1935 arms & motto

Arun District Council
1976 design

BOGNOR REGIS

1945 motto

Bognor Coats of Arms
As displayed on the cover of Newsletter No.8
January 1983

At the Council meeting on the 26th May 1935, approval of the design and motto was not the only item of importance on the agenda - smoking was banned from future meetings, and councillors and members of the public were to rise when the 'first citizen' entered the room. A further suggestion by Councillor S.W. Allen that a fanfare of trumpets should be sounded, failed to find favour. The civic heads were obviously proud of their new emblem of dignity : they accorded a "hearty vote of thanks" to Commander Hudson and a few months later accepted a quotation from W.A. Baker Ltd., for the supply of a bronze plaque of the Arms for the front of the Town Hall, at a cost of £19.17.6d. They permitted the arms to be reproduced by the Austin Motor Company in their new ambulance brochure in 1937, and upon the coverlet of a cot dedicated to the Southern Railway Servants' Orphanage at Woking, by the Bognor Branch of that organisation in 1938.

Their enthusiasm was short-lived. The motto 'Action' ("it must be remembered" said the 'Post', "that there are bad as well as good actions") was also the title of the newspaper issued by Sir Oswald Mosley's 'blackshirts' of which Hudson was a member. He was present at a meeting addressed by Mosley at Bognor's Theatre Royal on 18th February 1940. Practically the entire police force of Bognor were on hand while Mosley, "aided by two sips from a glass of water", spoke for nearly three hours. When those in the gallery burst into 'for he's a jolly good fellow' at the mention of Churchill, he instructed his stewards to "take note of everyone who is interrupting and put them out next time." Following a clamp-down on Fascists, including Hudson, the Council in July recommended that the motto 'Action' be deleted from the coat of arms where appearing on the Council's vehicles, notepaper, etc., a move approved by the College of Arms in September.

Soon after D-Day four years later, the good townsfolk were invited to submit ideas for a new town motto (how tempting!). The winner was Mr. Arthur J. Edkins of 1, Westway, with 'To Excel', which endured until Bognor Regis lost its Urban District Council in 1974. Arun District Council. after twice rejecting a ludicrous design submitted by the Windsor Herald of the College of Arms, which included an "insanely grinning visor", finally plumped for the coat of arms in current use, chosen from drawings submitted by Councillor Peter Norton of Bognor Regis. In October 1975, Arun Council approved the addition of "between £400 and £700" to the £654 already set aside for the design and provision of a new coat of arms, without a motto.

As far as demolition goes, the town has lived up to both its mottoes. Today, Bognor Town Hall still displays the 1935 coat of arms with the post-war motto, and others appear equally reluctant to change the old order. In 1964, the town clerk was taking issue with local shopkeepers, because. manufacturers of souvenirs were still using Bognor's 1890's-version town crest thirty years after its replacement. I've not had a look in 1982, but on a wander round the local souvenir shops the previous summer, I spotted bookmarks, plastic pennants and crested cutlery, all bearing not only the 1935 Bognor coat of arms, but also the motto 'Action'! While it is heartening to see that Bognor still retains her own identity, (so far, Arun lettered rock hasn't put in an appearance) it does seem unfortunate that the suppliers, Messrs Colourmaster, are perpetuating a motto which contributed so much in its day to the joke image of Bognor.

Sources
Bognor Regis Post, 27/10/34, pp3, 16; 30/3/1935, pp 1,3,9;
               24/2/1940, p 2; 3/10/1964, p.10.
Bognor Regis Observer, Jan/Oct.1975.
Sussex County Magazine, Vol.9 (1935) pp 136, 396.
B.R.U.D. Council Minutes, 431,720,1390,(1935); 1042(1937); 1840(1938);
               461,484,616, (1940); 439 (1944); 395 (1945)

....

"A Most Shocking Accident"
(Newsletter No.10, January 1984)

Beside the main path in South Bersted churchyard, near the west end of the church, is a tombstone bearing the following (now barely legible) inscription -

**In Memory of Louisa
daughter of Edmund and Mary Peachey,
who was unfortunately killed
by the sweep of a windmill,
May 25th, 1827, in the 4th year of her age.**

**Here innocence with beauty lies,
.....d from Earth to kindred skies.
Short was her life, her Death severe
.... the paternal tear.**

The sad tale is recounted in the 'Brighton Gazette' of May 31st 1827:-

"CHICHESTER - A most shocking accident happened on Friday last to a child about three years and a half, the daughter of Edmund Peachey, Old Broyle Mill, near this city. It appears that the child went out to play with an elder sister, and finding the mill door open, went in and got out on the stage, as it is supposed, in search of the miller.

The sails were going round rapidly at the time, one of which struck her on the back part of the head and precipitated her through the railings to the ground, a distance of about twenty yards. The child was instantly taken up, but without the least sign of life. It was found that the skull was fractured. An inquest was held upon the body on Saturday. Verdict - Accidental Death."

The 1846/7 Tithe Map and schedule for the parish of St. Peter the Great, Chichester (West Sussex Record Office) shows a windmill at Broyle roughly where Mill House. east of Canterbury Close, now stands

....

THE HAZARDS OF SEA BATHING IN VICTORIAN BOGNOR
(Newsletter No.11, July 1984)

In the early 18th Century, when English 'Society' in the wake of Royal patronage, began to desert the inland spa in favour of the new seaside 'watering places', men and women not only consumed quantities of sea water for medicinal purposes, but bathed together devoid of clothing. The activities of gentlemen 'lookers on' armed with telescopes, however, soon led to female bathers donning long flannel cloaks, and to the invention of the horse-drawn bathing machine to transport them further into the waves away from the public gaze.

The horror with which the Victorians, a century later, viewed the practice of mixed as well as nude bathing, was far more than a response to voyeurism.. It is readily dismissed as yet another example of the proverbial Victorian hypocrisy - a desire to cover up or avoid all that was 'nasty' in society - people did not possess bodies, just as the labouring classes did not suffer appalling conditions of housing and sanitation.

Any open discussion of taboo subjects was halfway to acceptance; hence local newspapers referred coyly to "indelicate" infringements of the bathing regulations and to "an occasional bathing system obnoxious and highly discreditable" (1)

The Marxist historian will argue further that here was an attempt, by those who dictated public behaviour and enforced the law, to keep the 'lower orders' in their place, a case of 'do as we say, not as we do'. For the development of a railway network, the introduction of 'penny-a-mile' Parliamentary trains in 1845 and the Bank Holiday Act of 1871, rendered these hitherto retreats of the fashionable and well-to-do, accessible to the hordes from the industrial and rural areas. What had been carte-blanche behaviour for the idle rich could no longer be tolerated as part of the plebeian pursuit of pleasure. But this 'rush into the sea' took place on an unprecedented scale, and strict segregation of the sexes may have been partly an over-reaction by Victorian guardians of public morality, in an age that had witnessed many threats to public order.

There was also the Evangelical influence on morals. Just as today's grin and bare it philosophy is to some extent a reaction to Victorian stuffiness, so too was the resurgence of puritanism and Christian ethics in the 19th Century a passive revolt against the licentiousness and tide of contagious immorality of the Regency period. 'Cleanliness next to godliness' had little to do with the brand of soap one used.

Whatever the motives, morality decency, modesty and legality became confused. The bathing-machine - originally an 'optional extra' for those who wished to protect their modesty - became the only refuge allowed by local bye laws for bathers with or without costumes. Yet even Victorian beaches enjoyed a freedom that was generally unacceptable; like today, nudity was considered respectable if it was far enough off the beaten track. An 1868 Guide-book informed visitors to Bognor that secluded Felpham was "a good place for bathing without the machine .... where custom has very conveniently assigned one retired spot for the use of ladies" (2).

Bognor (reputedly Britain's first resort specially created by one man for the purpose of sea-bathing) dragged its feet in getting going as a resort, but was less slow in introducing bathing regulations, once an 1822 Act of Parliament had established a Local Board of Commissioners. A decade and a half earlier, the resort's first guide book claimed: "no particular place has been allotted .... to female bathers. Men and women indiscriminately resort to the eastern side of the Hotel" (3) - the Hotel being situated at the foot of West Street. The 1822 Act, however, stipulated:

"And whereas the Practice of Undressing on the Sea Beach, and bathing in the Sea .... has been and is a great Annoyance to the Inhabitants and Visitors thereof ....if any Person or Persons shall undress on the Sea Beach, or shall bathe Undressed in the Sea, except from a Bathing Machine between the village of Aldwick and the westernmost of the Felpham Groynes, he, she, or they, shall for each and every offence, forfeit and pay .... the sum of Twenty Shillings" (4).

The failure of the Act to pinpoint exactly where Aldwick began and Bognor ended in 1822, meant that 51 years later the Clerk of the Local Board had to peruse the parish maps and question "one or two old inhabitants" before deciding that a case of indecent bathing was beyond the Board's jurisdiction (5).

In 1825, the town crier was directed to give notice to the inhabitants "against the practice of Bathing and exposing their persons on the shore within the limits prescribed by the Act" (6) and at intervals thereafter the Clerk was instructed to issue handbills to the same effect. Otherwise, records of the Board's proceedings before 1867 are few, and the *West Sussex Gazette*, the first local newspaper to report prosecutions in any depth, did nor appear until 1853.

With the arrival of the railway in 1864, the town and its popularity began to spread and steps had to be taken to preserve its reputation as "a thorough specimen of a respectable watering place - very quiet, very clean and perhaps somewhat dull to visitors expecting to find the gaieties usually provided at such places" (7). To the growing number of private girls' schools in the town, the attraction of 'safe bathing' had to mean more than a gently sloping foreshore. Any rowdy and disruptive elements who might lower the tone were to be discouraged, so that when in 1872 the Local Board:

> "anticipated that a large number of Excursionists would visit the town
> on the following Sunday, the Clerk was requested to call the attention
> of the Police to the necessity of their preventing any bathing from the
> shore except from the Bathing Machines...." (8).

THE BEACH AND ESPLANADE, EAST OF PIER.

Two years later, on learning that the Clerk to the recently opened Merchant Taylors' Convalescent Home had misinformed the Government Inpsector regarding an alleged case of typhoid in the town, a needled Local Board Chairman retaliated by referring to

"many of the patients spitting and using bad language on the promenade, and causing much annoyance by exposing their wounds on
the shore when they went to bathe." (9):

On the bathing front, things livened up in the 1870s. "Disgraceful" and "disgusting"
were epithets applied to the case of two men in June 1873, who were "only 10 or 15
yards from the Esplanade, bathing at 2 o'clock without drawers"; one who appeared
before the Board to apologise was fined ten shillings, and his companion fifteen
shillings (10). Three months later, Messrs Horace Savory and George Molineux
Smallpiece appeared before Chichester County Bench. This time the charges were
dropped after Mr. Malim for the defence pointed out that bathing had occurred at a
point away from houses between Clarence Road and Gloucester Road, and that the
nearest notices cautioning bathers were at Felpham, a quarter of a mile away. He also
"considered the Board were very misguided in bringing such an action; but the fact
was they had for their Chairman a reverend gentleman who was very anxious to court
popular applause, and so spoke in defence of the Poor" (11).

In 1875, as a result of the same reverend gentleman (the Rev. G.W. Fishbourne,
Congregational minister) witnessing a gentleman bathing from a ladies' bathing
machine, a bye-law was passed which stipulated:

"A person of the male sex above the age of ten shall not, while bathng,
approach within 100 yards of any place at which any person of the female
sex may be set down for the purpose of bathing" (12).

and vice-versa (the ten year age limit applied only to males). Bathing machines for
the two sexes were to be placed a minimum of 150 yards apart on 'stands' occupying
separate stretches of the foreshore: those for ladies between Clarence Road and the
Steyne, those for men between West Street and the town's boundary (these designated
areas changed over the years). Charges were fixed at 6d (2 1/2p) per half hour; or for
children, 6d under the care of an attendant, 4d if they shared a machine with other
children. For this fee, the proprietors were obliged to provide clean drawers for the
men, a clean gown for the ladies, and a clean towel for each adult and child.

The bathing machine proprietors were held equally responsible for any infringement
of the bye-laws on bathing. In addition, earlier bye-laws of 1868 (13), required them
to maintain their machines in good order and clean, safe condition; to ensure that
each machine was numbered on the back "in figures not less than two inches deep"; to
keep strictly to the stands appointed for his or her machine; to behave civilly at all
times to any "peace officer" or Board official; and not to charge excess fares. On

renewal of the licence for each machine every April, the owner had to be "well known to the Local Board, or provide a certificate under the hands of two respectable rated residents" equally well known and residing within five miles of the town.

In 1873 the owners of the Gentlemen's machines objected that the order to display copies of bye-laws 12 and 13 on the inside and outside of their machines, injured the paintwork (these bye-laws referred to the throwing of stones and rubbish upon the stands, and the provision of "woollen or cotton drawers" for male bathers) (14). Four years later, Mary Wheatland offended by plying for hire on a stand not allotted to her, and William Ragless for allowing a lady to bathe from a gentleman's machine. Charges were dropped, but in 1879 Ragless was fined a nominal shilling for a repeat offence, despite his plea that he did not bathe both sexes in the same machine, and such a regulation would force him to "shut up shop" (15).

THE BEACH, WEST OF PIER, AND ROYAL PIER HOTEL

As Mr. Pimlott asserts in 'The Englishman's Holiday' this combination of voluminous bathing attire for the ladies, the bathing machine, and the bye-laws, carrying a forty shilling fine, only "stressed what they desired to minmise" (16). Apart from the official Peeping Toms watching for any miscreants, a certain type of spectator was still proving an annoyance; by 1895 the telescope had been updated by:

"the multiplication of instantaneous cameras .... there are many cases of ladies who are positively afraid to emerge from the seaside machine or tent in which they don their bathing dress, on account of the nuisance" (17)

Such inquisitiveness was not the prerogative of the male sex - east of Gloucester Road, nude bathing for men was permitted on the understanding that "after breakfast hours, they will adopt costumes" (18). In 1900 complaints were made that "it is again a common recurrence for women to bring their big boys to bathe - and to stay and look on" (19).

Allowing males to bathe naked on designated stretches of beaches provided one argument against mixed bathing. In the closing years of Victoria's reign, however, the sea breeze of change was blowing over Britain's beaches. After decades of competing with each other in the degree of modesty they upheld, resorts were bracing themselves to allow mixed bathing in order to keep up with the times. Bognor must have been among the first, for in April 1899, the Urban District Council (which had succeeded the Local Board in 1895) granted a request by Mary Wheatland to allow mixed bathing on her side of the Pier - a privilege granted to the West side only the previous season - again on the understanding that "proper costumes" were worn. 'Mixed' of course, meant sharing the same stretch of shingle, but a few months later the parade inspector reported an instance of a man, woman and two children occupying the same machine. Council Chairman Curwen Sisterson, J.P. had however, "carefully enquired and ascertained that the 'guilty' party were respectably married with their own childrren. "Mixed bathing" , he maintained, "had been the making of the town this season and last. If people want to do wrong, they would not go to a bathing macine" (20).

The absurdity of the law, when members of the same family were unable to share the same machine without much ado, was clearly demonstrated here. But those who shared Mr. Sisterson's more liberal outlook ("I would rather trust the sinner than the saint") had to reckon with such killjoys as Dr. W. Gordon Stables, M.D.,R.N.. Writing in the *Bognor Observer's* 'Health and Home Column' in August 1904, he condemned as "shocking" and "shameless", the sight of "girls in their teens ... paddling in the sea with raised dresses as if they were mere mites of children. It is a disgrace to our modest Britain, although such women may be unmaidenly enough not to think so".

References

1.   *West Sussex Gazette,* 13th August 1868.
2.   A & C Black; *Where Shall We Go,* 1868, p.19.
3.   J.B. Davis; *The Origin & Description of Bognor or Hothamton* (London, 1807).
4.   3 Geo.IV c57; (West Sussex Record Office UD/BR/9/3/1).
5.   Minutes of the Bognor Local Board of Health, 2nd October 1873 (W.S.R.O.UD/BR/1/1).

6.   Minutes of the Commissioners, 4th July 1825 (W.S.R.O UD/BR/1/1A).
7.   A & C Black, op cit, p.18.
8.   Minutes of the Bognor Local Board of Health, 4th July 1872 (W.S.R.O. UD/BR/1/1).
9.   *West Sussex Gazette* 25th June 1874.
10.   Ibid, 10th July 1873.
11.   Ibid, 4th September 1873.
12.   1875 Byelaws, no.5 (W.S.R.O. UD/BR/9/3/1).
13.   W.S.R.O. UD/BR/9/3/1).
14.   Minutes of the Bognor Local Board of Health, 17th July 1873 (W.S.R.O. UD/BR/1/1).
15.   Ibid, 16th August 1877 and 20th Sept. 1877 (W.S.R.O. UD/BR/1/2).
        West Sussex Gazette 14th August 1879.
16.   J.A.R. Pimlott; *The Englishman's Holiday* Harvester Press, 1976 pp.128 130).
17.   *Bognor Observer* 11th September 1895
18.   Abel Heywood & Sons; *Guide to Bognor.*
19.   "75 Years Ago", *Bognor Regis Observer,* 1/8/1975.
20.   *Bognor Observer,* 6th September 1899.

Note : *Mixed Sea Bathing in Victorian Bognor* is a more detailed study on the subject produced for a Portsmouth Polytechnic Diploma in 1985. A copy is in W.S.R.O. MP.3188.

....-

THE GHOSTS OF UPPER BOGNOR
(Newsletter No.13, August 1985)

The reported sighting in March by local resident, Mr. Graham Bell, of the ghosts of a woman, a young boy and three King Charles spaniels near the duck pond in Hotham Park, brings to mind other stories relating to the house and grounds when privately owned by the Fletcher family.

In the mid 1970s, when David Allam and I were researching the house and it's past occupants, the daughter of a former domestic told us that after the death of John Ballett Fletcher in 1863, his widow, Sarah, lived the life of a recluse for the next 36 years, never venturing out in her carriage without the blinds drawn and her face veiled. and in the habit of taking a 'secret walk' in the grounds behind the house; an area from which the staff were strictly prohibited under threat of instant dismissal. Could the mysterious figures spotted by Mr. Bell have been the lonely Sarah with her youngest son, Edward, who died at an early age?

Before the house was rescued from demolition by Mr. Singer in 1977, I was asking the Park Attendant (or was he a Parade Inspector?) whether he received many enquiries from visitors about the building's history; whereupon he recounted the following story, which he had heard from a student minister of the Mormon Church and which I jotted down on a scrap of paper.

When one of the maids of the household became pregnant during an affair with the head gardener, he tried to abort the baby with a drug and killed her. A visiting relative of Fletcher heard of this, whereupon the gardener laid a curse on the relative, who later killed himself on the balcony with a knife which had been brought from Africa. The ghost of the relative and maid can still be seen, so it is said, between the balcony and conservatory garden which fronted the south side of the house.

None of the characters are named in this grisly and implausible little tale, which could have occurred at any time during the Fletcher 'reign' from 1857 to 1941, and which seems to have remained a remarkably well-kept secret - from whence did the Mormon student glean his information? (I too am guilty of failing to note the name of my informant !)

A few years ago, a 'peculiar atmosphere' in a 'particular spot' of the park was noted by four students of Bognor Regis College in a letter to the *Bognor Regis Post*; but until this year, apparently, nothing has materialised in the park itself. 'Things', however, have made their presence felt in the immediate vicinity.

In January 1946, the *Post*, with spooky introduction, carried the story of 'The girl in the Crinoline - Mystery of the Upper Bognor Road':-

As the wind howled through the naked branches of the sombre trees which overhang the Upper Bognor Road, and rain-laden clouds scurried across the darkened skies last Friday night (4th Jan.) 36 year-old Mr. Charles Frank Turrell ..... claims that he saw the figure of an early nineteenth century lady standing, sheltered by a bush, in the entrance drive to one of the large houses on the north side of the road. She was aged between 27 and 30 years, her dark-coloured crinolne was matched by a wide-brimmed bowl-shaped hat, and her black hair fell away in two loops over her forehead ...... her whole figure was illuminated by a shimmering light.

Mr.Bell's recent apparition, too, was bathed in a blue light and the woman dressed in what he took to be 18th century costume "with a wide-brimmed hat and long green dress".

Within half an hour, Mr. Turrell (on his bike) hurried back to the scene - but the figure had disappeared. He then realised that the lamp on the other side of the roadway (it was gas lamps in 1946) was not casting any light on the bush!

A peaceful Upper Bognor Road, pre-1900. Beyond the triangle of trees on the left (removed in 1956) is the original gate-lodge to the Fletcher estate, now Hotham Park.

'Legend has it', added the *Post*, 'that a certain house in Upper Bognor Road is haunted. Perhaps the wraith had wandered from its domicile to bewail the loss of the fine old trees on the Fletcher estate'. Until the late '40s, Upper Bognor Road included the stretch now known as High Street, down to Gloucester Road, but the last sentence suggests that the event occurred in the area now occupied by the College.

The *Post* re-ran the Crinoline Lady story in 1954, adding that she had never (to their knowledge) been seen before 1946 or since. The original report, however, prompted two responses a week later.

Visiting a house on the night of January 13th 'D.A.K.' and a friend had fled down the Upper Bognor Road after being 'surprised by the ghost lady walking towards us down the drive'. D.A.K., though, ended on a fanciful note - '.......she was not dressed as described by Mr. Turrell. As far as I could make out, all the lady wore was black negligee'! (Wishfull thinking?)

On another page, Mrs. J. Ridgers of Mordington Cottage, Mead Lane, recalled the strange experience of her late husband, Mr. George Leary. His apparition had been more substantially clothed.

> *Returning home from a card party late one night in 1900, he saw the "hooded figure of a woman glowing with a bluish light"* as she walked towards him. *Silently the glowing figure brushed past him and disappeared into some wooded land near the River Rife bridge.*

In a note on haunted houses in April 1949, columnist Morton Swinburne again reiterated the tradition of a haunted house in Upper Bognor Road, as well as one in the High Street, which had since become a shop, and an 'unlucky' house in Sudley Road (all unidentified). This prompted a letter from Miss V. Stevenson Sams regarding 'another Georgian residence'.

> *Prior to the war, I lived there for a number of years, and during that time, strange, unaccountable phenomena occurred. Shortly before leaving the house, I learnt from an acquaintance who knew the house well, that it had been reputedly haunted for some years. Another interesting fact that came to light was the one-time existence of a secret passage between the house and Aldwick Manor - now Hotham House.*

In the true tradition of such passages, Miss Sams added that as far as she knew, 'the exact whereabouts .... has never been discovered'. And the house? Kelly's street directories reveal that prior to 1937 a Virley Stevenson Sams resided at Sudley Lodge.

'Unaccountable phenomena' sound less substantial than Mr. Turrell's illuminated lady. In February 1954, Mrs. Brownie Peabody ('well-know in local stage circles') recalled something in-between. During a honeymoon spent at 'Naldera', Sea Road, Felpham, in July 1949, she and her husband went to a dance at Bognor. Missing the last bus home, they walked back along the north side of the main road.

As we were crossing the Upper Bognor Road by Hotham Park, I heard a swishing sound and, looking across at the wall opposite, saw the shadow of what looked like a man. It was moving towards Felpham.

The shadow, headless, remained in motion when the couple stood still, 'so it couldn't have been our shadows'. On recounting their story at breakfast next morning, the landlady replied, "Oh, you've seen our ghost. I bet it didn't have a head." One wonders how a headless shadow could even vaguely be identified as 'what looked like a man' !)

Since the 1940s, with the annual depletion of shady trees and the transformation of Upper Bognor Road into a fluorescently lit race-track, it is only to be expected that ghosts, shadowy or radiant, with or without heads, have sought the more secluded confines of the park around midnight. I wouldn't be surprised though, to read one of these days of the sudden re-appearance in 'Hotham Way' of dear old Sir Richard himself. After all, commemorating his name in a new four-lane flyover is enough to provoke him to rise from, let alone turn in, his grave - complete, no doubt, with the 'white hair, white eyes and white hands', which Lady Jersey so affectionately described in her letter to Edward Jerningham in 1796 !

Sunday 18th January 1987 -
HOW WE CELEBRATED BOGNOR'S BIRTHDAY
(Newsletter No. 16, February 1987)

Memorandum
1787.

January 18th 1787 - The first Foundation Stone of a Public Bathing Place at Bognor in the Parish of Berstead was laid by Sir Richard Hotham Knt. at the House called by the name of the Lodge.

Bognor's beginning - 1787. Memorandum of stone-laying (Bognor Lodge) in
South Bersted parish register.

Just before noon on the Great Day, a dozen and a half of us jostled for space outside the Town Hall. "Oh Yez, Oh Yez, hear ye, good citizens .....", bellowed the Town Crier, Mr. Charles Loake, shattering the Sunday silence. Good citizens and bad peered nervously from nearby windows. From the balcony the Mayor, Mrs. Pat Stinchcombe, accompanied by the Town Council's Clerk and bravely attired in period costume in sub-zero temperatures, delivered her civic greeting. On the hour a maroon flare (distress call for Bognor Regis?) soared high into the wintry sky. We all (at least three dozen by now) sang "Happy Birthday Bognor Regis", and Mr. Jim Brooks of BRAVO handed round promotional 3-tone sticks of lettered rock to the children

At 2pm a great multitude - 60? 70? - assembled at South Bersted Church. The Vicar, the Rev. Hugh Pruen, addressed the congregation. "On March 21st 1799, one of my predecessors, the Rev. Thomas Durnford, stood at the entrance by which you all entered today to receive the body of Richard Hotham .... We come here today as heirs and as trustees of the town he founded..... Let us pray for Bognor.... " A short reading by the Mayor. Three hymns: 'Praise my Soul the King of Heaven', 'I vow to Thee my Country' and Blake's 'Jerusalem'. A ten-minute slide-show by John Hawkins demonstrated the failure of past heirs & trustees, but closed on a note of hope for the future; then out into the chill air to lay our wreaths upon the snow-covered grave of "St. Richard", as the aptly named 'Promotor' newspaper dubbed him the following Wednesday.

3.30pm was the appointed time for the tree-planting ceremony in Hotham Park and at 3.25 some duly arrived, to find. the said ceremony completed. Made mental note: news-sheet editor in December 2036 to add "approx" beside timing of all New Year outdoor events. Witnessed replacement of Quercus suber sapling in its pot to wait warmer weather - as must the remainder of 'Bognor 200' festivities.

> Oh Tricky Sir Dicky, how rash you were
> To lay your stone so early in the year;
> Our expected brass-band had cold feet, we hear
> But brass monkeys aside, we gave you a cheer!

....

BOGNOR BEFORE HOTHAM
(Newsletter No.16, February 1987)

(The following merely scratches the surface of a subject into which others more learned have delved far deeper.)

Bognor was first recorded in a charter (Cartularium Saxonicum) of 680 AD as 'Bucganora', i.e. 'Bucge's ora'. In Old English, 'Bucge' was a woman's name (possibly a land-owner) and 'ora' means 'shore', in this case a beach or landing place, probably chosen for the protection afforded by the reef of Bognor Rocks. 'Ora' in coastal names is common in this region - e.g. Keynor, near Sidlesham (possibly 'Cymenesora', the initial landing place of the South Saxons in 477 AD), Itchenor, and Copnor near Portsmouth. Elsewhere it has a meaning 'hill slope', as in Bignor, below the South Downs ridge; or 'estuary' or 'river bank', as in Windsor (1).

Medieval Bognor had its own chapel, dedicated to St. Bartholomew. Writing in 1872 (2), Dudley Elwes cites a terrier (early land register) of South Bersted dated 10th March 1626, which lists among property of the vicarage an acre of land on the north side of the windmill at Bognor. In a footnote he adds that the windmill had "long since" been washed away by the sea which now (1872) formed the southern boundary of the said acre. Lindsay Fleming (3) suggests that since the mill may have been that depicted in early views of Bognor at the east end of the shore, St. Bartholomew's chapel may have stood somewhere south of the present eastern parade. Pure speculation! Two of our members Mr. & Mrs. Page, however, recently queried with me the origin of Church Path, which runs in a dead-straight line north from Lyon Street. Is it possible that this path once led sea-wards to the site of Bognor's chapel?

Detail from John Speed's map of Susssex, 1610

Mr H.L.F. Guermonprez records in S.A.C. (4), the discovery of a hoard of Bronze Age palstaves during the making of the Marshall Avenue estate in 1924. He then proposes that the southern part of Nyewood Lane was once an ancient trackway which followed the line of the present footpath across the Marshall estate to South Bersted, thence via Lidsey and Eartham to Upwaltham and Petworth. If one continues Church Path northwards, it would join the above trackway at the junction of Highfield and Shripney Roads.

Other archaeological finds indicate early occupation of the Bognor area. Among these are Roman and British coins found on the shore between Pagham and Bognor in 1841/2 (5), and more off Bognor in 1963 (6). The first 'dig' in the Bognor area, in 1965, revealed a Roman-British farmstead near Innerwyke Manor, Felpham. Ten years later, the only Iron Age settlement so far known on the coastal plain west of the Arun, was revealed during building of the housing estate between Rowan Way and Oak Grove - hence 'Bronze Close' and 'Stoneage Close' today!

Fleming's 3-volume work on Pagham contains a number of references to medieval Bognor. In 1279, for example, Nicholas de Scardevile, chaplain of Bognor's chapel, was one of three suspected of murdering William Lewyne of Bognor. Another resident, John Doreundel, was also murdered in the same year (7). Good service in the war of France - including the Battle of Crecy - won Robert atte Crouche of 'Boggenore' a pardon in January 1347 for his wrongdoings (8). And in 1538, workmen 'mending the ways' overheard a disloyal remark by William Hamlyn, who was placed in the stocks in the tithing of Bognor (9).

Thmas Yeakell and William Gardner's survey of Sussex, 1778.

Bognor Rocks, first mentioned in Court Rolls of 1493 as 'Le Rokke de Bogenore' and depicted on Speed's map of Sussex in 1610, are not, as legend has it, the site of early Bognor. Nevertheless, coastal erosion has taken its toll: in 1465, this and "other divers causes" had so reduced the tithing of Bognor and income from same, that the chapel of Bognor was merged with the vicarage of Bersted (10) and abandoned as a place of worship. In an interesting article on the coastline of Sussex (11), Mr. A. Ballard deduces from a comparison between Yeakell & Gardner's map of 1778 and the 6 in. O.S. map of 1875, a loss to the sea of 158 yards in a century. The early 19th century saw the disappearance of Bognor Common Brook, which stretched from West Street to Felpham Rife along the shoreline, and, but for Hotham's creation of a resort here and the subsequent erection of sea defences, Bognor might well by now have ceased to exist.

Sources
(1) Mawer & Stenton (eds) *The Place Names of Sussex*
        vol.1 (Camb. U.P. 1929)
        W.H.F. Nicholaisen (ed) *The Names of Towns & Cities in Britain*
        (Batsford 1970)
(2) *Sussex Archaeological Collections*, Vol.24, p.167.
(3) Lindsay Fleming, *History of Pagham* (1949), p. 605-6.
(4) *S.A.C.* vol.66, pp 225-31.
(5) *S.A.C.* vol.1, pp 26-31. This and other articles are referred
        to in Fleming, op cit, vol,2, pp 622-5
(6) *Bognor Regis Post*, 14th Sept. & 26th Oct. 1963.
(7) Fleming, op cit, vol.1, p 39.
(8) Ibid, pp52, 136.

(9)   Ibid, pp 136-7.

(10)   Ibid, p.117.

(11)   *S.A.C.* vol.53, pp 6-25. Fleming, op cit (vol.2 p. 548)
       claims 60 yards as a truer figure.

....

WAS BOGNOR HOTHAM'S SECOND CHOICE?
(Newsletter No.17, August 1987)

I am indebted to Mr. Charles Butler who, in his research on Bognor's founder, Sir Richard Hotham, unearthed the following extract from R. Scott's *A Topographical and Historical Account of Hayling Island,* published by I. Skelton, in Havant in 1826; republished by Frank Westwood, The Petersfied Bookshop, in 1974:-

'The attractive powers and capabilities of this charming place (Hayling Island) have never been questioned, but the property having been for generations strictly entailed in the family bearing the honours of the earldom of Arundel Castle, its advantages could not be enjoyed by the public. We have been informed that Sir Richard Hotham, the enterprising founder of Bognor, first chose this delightful spot for carrying his building designs into execution; but was disheartened, and ultimately obliged, with reluctance, to abandon his views, in favour of Bognor, from the then dangerous state of the northern approach to the Island, and the property being so firmly fettered by the "STATUTE OF GREAT MEN." The legal spell is, however, at length dissolved, an Act having been passed in the last Session of Parliament for vesting the Manor, Rectory, and Isle of Hayling, with all their royalties, immunities, and privileges, in the present possessor, who intends, we understand, to adopt the views of Sir Richard, and to engraft upon them all the improvements which the liberal and extended ideas of the age can bestow......'

Until now, it has been the general belief that Hotham first conceived the idea of creating his own purpose-built bathing resort following his defeat at Southwark in the General Election of July 1784 and a chance visit to Bognor, as a convalescent, that summer. The evidence above, however, suggests that Hotham had been toying with the idea for some time and exploring other possible sites along the South Coast before his arrival here. Further research on ths subject - at the Hampshire County Record Office for instance - would be well worthwhile.

- 49 -

OWER GUIDING LIGHT

(Newsletter No.19, July 1988)

To evening strollers on Bognor's 'prom', the flashing of the Owers light, every thirty seconds on the distant horizon, is an object of curiosity. To local fishermen and the crews of Channel vessels, however, it spells an invaluable warning to steer clear of the maze of rocks and shallows, known as the Owers, that extend south and east of the Selsey peninsula. Nowadays a navigational buoy serves the purpose, but it was 200 years ago this year that the first Owers lightship was moored 9 1/2 miles off the Bognor coast and 7 miles south-east of Selsey Bill, at a position of Latitude 50 43 N, Longitude 0 37 W (1).

The 'Owers' lightship station was, I believe, the third to be established by Trinity House; today there are over forty (2), but the first was installed without the Elder Brethren's approval. Robert Hamblin, a barber of Lynn who married a shipmaster's daughter and became manager of a collier, recognised the problem of distinguishing one lighthouse from another. In 1730 he was granted a 14-year patent by the King, for his idea of stationing lightships at dangerous coastal positions, each identifiable by a different arrangement of lanterns. A year later his partner in the project, David Avery, moored the first light vessel close to the Nore buoy in the Thames estuary. Contrary to the opinion of Trinity House, this proved a boon to mariners, and shipowners willingly subscribed to its upkeep. Fearing the indiscriminate placing of more lightships, Trinity House obtained the revocation of Hamblin's patent, but after an outcry from mariners and a concilliatory approach from Avery, they obtained their own patent in perpetuity and granted him a 61-year lease from 1733 at a rent of £100 (3).

The demand for lightships grew, and in 1788 a vessel costing £4,500 (4) was moored two miles south of the Owers shoal, which consists of the Malt Owers, Middle Owers, Outer Owers, etc.. 'Owers' is thought to have the same derivation as the 'or' in Bognor, meaning 'bank', 'shore' or 'landing place'; and may possibly be the 'ora' in 'Cymenes-ora', the landing place of the South Saxons in A.D.477 (5). Here, too, is the probable site of the cathedral built by St. Wilfrid in the 7th century; the see was transferred to Chichester in 1071. Between the Mixon beacon one mile out to sea and the Outer Owers some 4 to 5 miles out, runs a channel known as the Looe Stream ('Looe' - as in Cornwall - is Celtic, meaning 'inlet of water' or 'pool'). Centuries ago this flowed through a medieval deer-park - an area still marked on shipping charts today as 'The Park'. At low tide the Owers rocks are covered by only a few feet of water flowing very swiftly into the Looe Stream and resembling a tidal mill-race. Before the arrival of the lightship, beacons lit upon the headland provided the only warning of these perilous waters, and it wasn't until 1861 that a lifeboat station was established at Selsey. By 1807 the lightship had become something of a tourist attraction: Bognor's first guide-book was recommending to visitors:

"An excursion to the Oar Lights .....would be very agreeable. Some ships having been lost upon this coast, it was deemed necessary to keep a vessel at anchor with large lanthorns hoisted aloft at night and a red flag during the day ..... " (6)

An early Ower's Lightship vessel. (WS.R.O. F/PD.45)

There are no reliable records of the earlier Owers lightships. A history of the 'Owers' which appeared in the Bognor Post of 23rd December 1922 (repeated in 1980) claimed that the vessel then present was the third to be stationed there, but also stated that the first had arrived in 1738 and was replaced by a 'more seaworthy craft' in 1764 although Trinity House has confirmed 1788 as the initial date. In general, early hulls were of oak and the warning lights were large lanterns swung from the yard-arm, fitted originally with wax candles which were superceded by oil lamps and later, electricity. Later lanterns included reflectors swinging in gimbals, which maintained a steady and horizontal beam in rough seas. The distinguishing lighting characteristics of each ship were set out in the Admiralty 'List of Lights'. When the revolving light was installed at the Owers isn't known (the first of any lightship was in 1827) but the West Sussex Gazette of 26th June 1873, reporting the installation of the 'melancholy' foghorn, gives an indication:

> "Since the revolving light has been, with the new Owers Light Ship, adopted off our coast, a further improvement has been adopted on board, which has a novel rather than a pleasing effect on the ears of the inhabitants. This is the use of the fog-horn which, through the sea-mist arising, was used nearly the whole of Sunday last."

Hardly an 'improvement' for crew members attempting to sleep amid the deafening blast! According to the *Post* report of 1922, two 9 h.p. two-cylinder internal combustion engines supplied the compressed air used in fog for sounding the siren and knolling the submarine bell. The latter was lowered to a depth of 18 ft. and sounded seven times every seven seconds, and the siren, one long blast each thirty seconds

Other details, 'received from the crew' in 1922, read as follows (corresponding dimensions of the steel-hulled vessel which took over in 1947 - known as Number 3 Lightvessel in the Admiralty 'List of Lights' - have been added in brackets):-

> "The mast is of steel and it is 68 (59) ft. from the water-line to the globe at the top of the mast .... the lantern itself is 37 (40) ft. from the water-line   It has 7 lamps, showing red and white alternatively every 30 seconds. The lantern is kept in motion by a large clock. The ship is 110 (137) ft. long, 20 (25) ft. in breadth and stands 10 (15) ft, out of the water. She is moored by the bows to a 60 cwt. anchor by a chain which is 1 5/8 inches thick and 210 fathoms long. In normal weather the ship rides with 90 to 100 fathoms of chain out, keepng the remainder to be paid out according to the severity of the climatic conditions. The cable is fitted with a swivel every 45 fathoms to prevent the chain from becoming entangled when the ship swings with the turn of the tide and wind.

> The crew consists of the captain, 2 lamplighters (one of whom takes over the cooking), 2 fog-signal drivers and 2 seamen ... . There is a spacious forecastle, in which six members of the crew sleep, dine and cook their food. Each man prepares his own food, which is then placed in a steamer to be looked after by the lamplighter acting as cook. There are in all eleven members of the crew, including the men temporarily at work in the store ashore. On the 1st of each month, 4 men from the

store relieve 4 men who have completed 2 months on board. The captain is relieved every month. The men have to serve until the age of 60 before being entitled to a pension. The crew have to find their own food and clothing, with the exception of a cap, jumper and collar."

I doubt whether the crew would have described their accommodation aboard as 'spacious', but at least they enjoyed more space and company than a lighthouse keeper. 'Stand-easy' hours were often occupied by rope or cloth mat-making, model-making and other crafts, or reading. At Christmas the isolated crew were not forgotten by the inhabitants of Bognor and Selsey. The following report, for example, appeared in the Bognor news of the *West Sussex Gazette* on New Year's Day, 1891:

"SEASONABLE GIFTS - The hardy salts who reside on the Owers Lightship off Bognor have great cause to bless the memory of the late Mr. Robert Mumford, who, for several years past, was instrumental in making Christmas a festive time among them. His custom was to give himself, and to collect money from his friends for the purpose of providing the men a sumptuous dinner on Christmas Day, and it seems as if this laudable practice is to be continued. This year the sum of

£3.11s. was collected, and expended on a goose, beef, ham, cheese, bread, potatoes, onions, and tobacco, supplemented with a gift of cigars all of which were conveyed to the lightship by one of the Bognor watermen. The isolated watchers on the deep received the gifts with great thankfulness, and expressed their grateful acknowledgement by letter to those who had thus ministered to their pleasure and comfort and in wishing them all the compliments of the season, trusted that, in seeking the well-being of others, their own happiness would be increased."

The 'Owers' has suffered the occasional mishap. Being moored in shallow water, the ship had a habit of breaking adrift, on one occasion reaching St. Valery-en-Caux on the French Coast. (7) On the night of 15th July 1924 in Cowes harbour, after a 3-month overhaul and with its valuable machinery and new provisions aboard, the moored lightship grounded and keeled over on its side as the tide fell. The rising tide entered the open ports and the ship lay almost submerged in harbour. The salvage vessel 'Trover' had the task of pumping out and raising it. (8)

In September 1973, the last Owers lightship, purpose-built by Philip & Son Ltd. at Dartmouth in 1947, was replaced (as many others have been since) by a 40 ft. high, 100-ton Lanby - a large Automatic Navigation Buoy. Economics and shortage of crews made this necessary; the estimated cost of the buoy, with shore control from St. Catherine's lighthouse, Isle of Wight, was said to be £20,000 as opposed to £500,000 for a new ship, with an annual maintenance bill of £30,000 reduced to £3,000. Once the buoy had served a probationary period, the lightship ended its 26-year vigil at the Owers, and was towed to Harwich to prepare for service elsewhere. (9)

Over the preceeding 185 years, there must have been many who owed their lives to the dedication of the 'Owers' crews during their two-monhly long shifts. The following is one such crew, who were present on the night of 3rd April 1881 and were listed on the.last page of the census return for Bognor (10) :-

1. Henry Skeats; married; age 49, Mate; from Newtown, Isle of Wight.
2. James Barry; married; age 37; Lamplighter; from Warsash, Hampshire
3. George Stone Comden; married; age 36; Lamplighter; from Grandbank, B.S., Newfoundland.
4   Edward Stephen Swift; married; age 26; Engine Driver; from Southampton.
5. Edwin L(?)uckett; married; age 30; Engine Driver; from Preston, Dorset
6. George Maskell; single; age 22; A.B. Seaman; from Ramsgate, Kent
7. William Davis; single; age 20; A.B. Seaman; from Portland, Dorset.

References

(1) Amiralty 'List of Lights' 1911. The lightship is also marked on the
Admiralty survey 'Owers to Dungeness', published at the Admiralty
1878, 4th edition 1920, WSRO, PM61.
(2) George Goldsmith Carter, *Looming Lights* (Reader's Union & Constable
1947); introduction by Sir Geoffrey Callender. page xv.
(3) I am indebted to the Information Officer of Trinity House Lightship
Service, Tower Hill, London, for kindly supplying historical
details of both the Owers and Nore lightships.
(4) Richard Woodman, *Keepers of the Sea* (Terence Dalton Ltd.,
Suffolk, 1983), p.35
(5) A Mawer & F M Stenton, *The Place Names of Sussex* (Cambridge U.P.,
1929), p.83, and W E P Done, *Looking Back in Sussex,*
Faber & Faber, 1953), pp 73-5.
(6) J B Davis, *The Origin & Description of Bognor or Hothamton*
(London 1807)
(7) Richard Woodman, op. cit.
(8) *Bognor Post,* 19 July 1924, p.1
(9) *West Sussex Gazette* 12 July 1973
Bognor Regis Post 7 July 1973 and
Bognor Regis Observer 28 Sept. 1973
(10) P.R.O. ref. RG11/1124, Folio 106.

....-

GOODBYE TO AN OLD FRIEND
- The Passing of 'The Post'
(Newsletter No.21, July 1989)

I have grown accustomed to writing obituaries on Bognor's old buildings, but is is
with greater saddness that I now record the death of our very own local newspaper.
Although preserved in memory in the newly-merged *Guardian & Post*, the *Bognor
Regis Post,* a mere shadow of its former self, ceased to exist as a newspaper in its
own right on 18th May 1989, after 67 years.

The first issue of the *Bognor Post* appeared on 7th January 1922. It was in May of
that year that the *Bognor Observer* celebrated fifty years in print - and mourned the
death of its founder, Henry Lovett, J.P.. By now, though, the *Observer* was
Chichester-based and the format had become, perhaps, a little stale and stereotyped.
The Post was a bright and breezy alternative.

urance
without

DICAL
[NATION.
ns reduced.
increased.

r the New
RD" POLICY,
d by the

ASSURANCE
COMPANY,

louse, Newgate St.,
on, E.C.4.
: 2a, The Parade,
load, Bognor.

The Bognor Post

EDITED BY HIRAM KNIGHT.

By Special

DYSON
(Late I
PIANO
PLAYEI
IMPORTERS, RE
BO(
Pianos and
or

[POSTAGE ONE PENNY.]   SATURDAY, FEBRUARY 18TH, 1922.   ONE

The founder of *The Post* was a Lincolnshire man, Mr Hiram Knight, whose journalistic career began with the *Northampton Evening Telegraph* and included a post-war spell as assistant news-editor and sports editor of the *Sunday Times*, sport being his self-confessed 'first love'.   Introducing himself to his first Bognor readers, he explained:

"All along it has been my fixed intention to produce a paper of my own and two years ago, when with my family, I first visited Bognor and fell in love with the town, the district and the people, I made up my mind that I would inflict myself upon them .... I have long held the view that the day of the old-fashioned local news sheet is passed for good or ill, and I advocate its being replaced with a replica of its more vigorous London contemporaries.   We are no longer in the eighteenth century, and papers must move with the times .... "

His first editorial continued in the same vein:

"Today we commence an enterprise which we venture to hope will meet a great need .... a 'live' newspaper, as distinct from a mere news and advertising sheet,   is an essential to the welfare of any localtiy and par- ticularly in this assertion applicable to a rapidly-growing community with an assured future ...... "

In its silver jubilee issue, *The Post* recalled the very first editorial meeting, between Mr Knight and his boyhood friends, Mr & Mrs K Davidson, who were about to move to Hothampton Court Hotel. In a half-empty flat over Gale's the outfitters in York Road (premises recently converted to office space by Staffurth & Bray), they discussed the first reports and editorial which the three had completed.

The new paper proved a great success. On March 18th., with a declared aim of "being the very best local paper in the kingdom", it recorded a rise in net sales from an initial 1,249 to 2,022 in two months, already exceeding its local counterparts.

Within eight pages (selling for one penny) the limited staff crammed a lot of news. The content was entertaining and informative, lively and unpredictable. Then, as now, you knew where to find everything and the page-size was manageable. First year features included a popular 'Book of Babble' - an anonymous satire on local affairs written in 'Biblical' style - and an exciting serial, 'The House of Sin' by Allen Upward, which ended abruptly in June, uncompleted! The Entertainments scene was penned initially by 'Lafan B Gay'. But from the start it was essentially a local newspaper, for and about Bognor people. Its founder urged a spirit of local patriotism: "Bognor must boom". The main issues in 1922 were a better rail service (for which Mr Knight corresponded personally with the Chairman of the L.B. & S.C.R.), high-pricing by local traders, and the continual Council wrangling over the running of the recently-erected Pavilion dance-hall. An "almost seraphic" peaceful debate in December, drew the comment: "That this was due to the regrettable absence of Mr Staffurth, through illness, must not be assumed ....."

In my own past forages among the files, I have encountered many instances of the same amused coverage of municipal affairs (e.g. following the granting of an official coat of arms in 1935: "In outward formality, at any rate, the Council should soon be the very model of what a Council should be"). *The Post* strove to present readers with fair and impartial reports, and to provide a platform for all to air their views, but it wasn't afraid to speak out when the occasion demanded. Successive editors waged campaigns against proposals they considered inappropriate for Bognor - such as funfairs for the eastern seafront in the early 1930s - or too expensive for the ratepayers, like a £53,000 bathing pool, every pro-pool candidate losing his seat at the election of April 1936. (Read also, the editorial comment of 19th June 1965, on the secrecy surrounding the sacking of the Town Clerk, Mr Paul Smith, which drew national attention and resulted in a public enquiry). During the war, *The Post* organised a 'Spitfire' fund and from August 1940 to April 1943 raised £2,660. The office and printing works of the Southern Post was itself badly blasted by a bomb which fell behind the building on Good Friday night, April 1941.

The paper's first office was in York Road Chambers, but very soon transferred to premises over a gramophone shop at No. 10 London Road. Early in 1923 a Little-hampton edition was begun, followed shortly by a Chichester edition. All three were printed by Mitchell & Co. in Arundel before more spacious and convenient offices and works were opened on the present London Road site in the summer of 1923.

Among Hiram Knight's team was Mr J W Blackman, responsible for the sporting notes and advertising. Mr Henry Mayo, who was also developing the Summerley Estate at Felpham was the first Managing Director until a fatal motor accident in March 1935. He was succeeded by Mr F W L Smithers, who had joined the firm as secretary in August 1923. Mr Smithers died in September 1974, aged 78, and Mr Jack Dobson took over. Hiram Knight resigned as editor in the autumn of 1924 and was succeeded by Mr Lewis Essex, a freelance author and journalist and ex-chairman of the Bognor Liberal Party. (I see he was responsible for a 17-page lyrical description of Bognor's charms in my copy of the 1926 official guide published by the Bognor Town Advertising Committee). During his one-year reign at *The Post*, he campaigned successfully for a police court at Bognor, only to becomne its first defendant, in a minor motoring case!

Mr Essex was replaced by Mr Robert T Rickards, himself a Fleet Street man and able writer, who in 1923 inaugurated the popular 'Leaves from my Notebook' feature, later headed by the familiar line drawing of leaves fluttering in a strong wind.

Ill-health prompted his resignation in February 1935, ten months before his death, and his place was taken by Mr Morton Swinburne. Mr Swinburne had entered journalism in the 1920s, following a career as a professional boxer. He was later boxing coach at Northcliffe School, Bognor Regis, during the head-ship of Mr Henry Colborne Brown and among the pupils was the Rt. Rev. David Sheppard, former England and Sussex opening batsman and now Bishop of Liverpool. Mr Swinburne's lifelong interest was natural history; he was elected a Fellow of the Zoological Society in 1938 and with Mr E M Venables was a founder of the Bognor Regis Natural Science Society that same year. He was licensee of the 'Cricketers Inn' at Westbourne from 1959 until shortly before his death in 1979 aged 82, having retired as editor of *The Post* in December 1966. Later editors were Mr H G Walgrove, whose impressive 52-year career also included news-editorships of the northern editions of Beaverbook Newspapers and various posts in Yorkshire, Liverpool and Suffolk; and from January 1977, Mr Robert Sears, formerly deputy-editor of the *East Grinstead Observer*.

Of all the journalists associated with *The Post*, probably the most celebrated was Mr Gerard Young, who joined the staff on January 2nd 1956 and produced 'Gerard Young's Column' for the next sixteen years.

Each week the reader learned something new about Bognor's colourful past or what was happening locally; Mr Young was also the paper's art critic, and very little escaped his attention. As his brother once said in a talk to our society, he always explained, often humourously, <u>why</u> he liked or disliked something; he stimulated as well as informed. One also sensed his influence on the newspaper itself; like Hiram Knight he wanted Bognor to sell itself, but by preserving, not destroying, the charm and individuality it still possessed. He awakened local apathy to the threat to demolish Hotham Park House, hoping it would one day house Bognor's unique but doomed museum collection. *The Post* organised an opinion poll on the issue - and a 'sixpenny fund' for the re-erection of the Jubilee Fountain in the Steyne. It's anti-'Butlin's stance at one time led to the banning of the paper within the camp's confines.

After Gerard Young's death in February 1972, *The Post* seemed to lose vitality. Mr Neville Nisse, ex-'showbiz' journalist and the driving force behind the Bognor Regis Town Twinning Association, injected some sparkle into its columns as deputy-editor between 1977 and 1984. In September 1985 the Bognor Regis Post Ltd. took over control from the Southern Post Ltd. and introduced a new-look *Post*. 'Printing' by new technology was no longer undertaken locally. In a last-ditch attempt to boost sales in October 1988, new owners, Sussex County Press, transformed the paper into a local version of the *News of the World*. The selling-price remained low: 12p from 1982, 15p since 1986.

The Post lacked the financial resources of its main rival, the *Bognor Regis Observer*, who unfairly distributed free copies locally. In an effort to compete with the genuine 'free' newspapers, *The Post* reduced itself to their illiterate level; it had become, in effect, the "mere news and advertising sheet" which Hiram Knight had been anxious to replace in 1922. "We seek to play our part as an independent critic of men and affairs. Of the measure of our success the public will form its own opinion," he had declared, "for the record of a newspaper is an open book". The final front page, with the banner headline 'On Yer Skates', and the inaccurate 'Your newspaper since 1923', said it all.

The Post was launched in an era when indeed, Bognor had "an assured future". Its demise coincides with the general decline of a town robbed of its good looks, its self-government and self esteem; a meeting place for clowns.

I pay tribute here to the countless backroom workers who have kept the presses of the *Bognor Regis Post* rolling over the years. Within the pages of 3,519 issues, it duly chronicled the life of the town and the people it served and championed so well; both the trivia and the big events, including those of sixty years ago, when Bognor became the centre of world attention. As such, its files are a happy hunting ground for the local historian. Thanks to the West Sussex Library Service, they are preserved on microfilm (with the exception of the first two years) and available to anyone who wishes to peruse them, at Bognor Regis Reference Library.

Sources:

Bognor Post, 1922 volume (in private ownership - my thanks for
the loan of same.
Bognor Regis Post, 11th January 1947,
My own collection of post-1960 newspaper cuttings.

....

BOGNOR - LET'S CHANGE IT !
(Newsletter No. 24, February 1991)

Amidst the recent condemnation of Arun District Council as the bogie-men of Bognor,
it was a welcome relief to read Mr Howard's letter to the local *'Observer'* in October
(1990), resurrecting an old theme. Businesses would fare better, he suggested, if the
town were to adopt the "pretty and appealing" name of 'Bellemer Regis' - or for ease,
'Belmer Regis'. But, as in the past, someone was quick to rebuff the very idea - 'belle-
mere' was French for stepmother, or mother-in-law, and would surely lead to greater
derision. Left to its own devices, Bognor would probably have long ago been
consigned to the history books by the ravages of the sea. But ever since Hotham the
Hatter dragged the place out of obscurity two centuries ago and rechristened it
'Hothamton', visitors and residents have maintained that Bognor's name was its
biggest handicap in making a name for itself - and have suggested equally
unattractive alternatives.'

In its Local Summary as far back as April 1900, the *West Sussex Gazette* was
asking:

> "Why Bognor? .... The name suggsts anything but the sweet, clean
> town which exists today with its unrivalled sands and yellow beach .
> .... Why not, if we look to the sylvan beauties of the country, to-
> wards Bersted, call it 'Elmslea', or, if the seafront is to be proclaimed,
> 'Beachton', 'Sandborough' or 'Groyneville suggest themselves. Again
> there are reasons why those who have worked for the place should be
> commemorated: in this conection some suggest 'Conderville'
> 'Longborough', or 'Staffurton' ....."

Those who were "in love with the first syllable" might call it 'Mudton', the *Gazette*
continued.

After a Christmas visit to Bognor in 1913, Thomas Beaney Cowtan wrote to the *Observer*. His conviction that Bognor's "ghastly" and "ugly" first syllable was preventing it from cashing in as a winter resort, was strong enough to launch him into verse:-

> Content is good, but wherefore rest
> Before you have attained the best?
> To you for Christmas I came down,
> But what a desolated Town!
> Though we despise the letter
> In truth remain the same:
> Your fortunes would be better
> If Bog-nor changed her name.
>
> This could be done with fitting tact,
> Till it emerged a fruitful fact;
> And folk would come for happy spells
> To her whose name alone repels;
> And with her friends of health and grace,
> Your hampered Town would take her place.
> When beauty greets the ear (and eye)
> You'll win your due prosperity!

This brought a spate of replies in January 1914. Wallis Arthur, the seaside summer showman who presented pierrot shows at the Olympian Gardens enclosure at the foot of Lennox Street, was the first, with his own poetic response entitled "No Change" :-

> If Bognor BE an ugly name
> Its lovers love it just the same,
> But talk of ugly names, an "out and out 'un"
> Is surely that of Thomas Beaney Cowtan.
> If BOG-NOR MUST be changed, and you arrange it,
> Please hear my prayer and don't to COW-TAN change it.

"Yours truly, Bognor" argued that 'Bog' in place-names and surnames wasn't all unplesasant and quoted a few somewhat obscure examples (Bog-omili were the friends of God, a religious sect, etc.). He went on:-

> Change if you like the names of some streets. Change if you can
> the general indifference to beauty, and architecture, which char-
> acterises so many buildings, etc., which are erected with little

if any architectural features, except it be those supposed to exist in the brain of an ordinary brick-builder. Induce if you can, the better class, the monied residents ......

And B.G. Best considered that BOGnor was no less unprepossessing than ROTTINGdean, SCARborough, RAMSgate or GRIMSby.

Captain H Arthur, of Sudley Road, was more interested in the origin of the town's name and proffered his own fanciful theory that 'Bagh-i-nur' in Persian, meaning 'Garden of Light', was a derivation aptly fitted to "this lovely little town". This inspired "K" to venture into the realms of fantasy with a tale of two Irishmen living in Bosham in A.D. 680 who visited the Roman brotherhood at 'Cissanceaster' and decided on a walk to the seaside. At low tide they set out to walk to an offshore reef of rocks -. got stuck in the wet sand and when dragged out shouted "Begorra, a bog", to which his Roman friend added "nomen orae" (the name of the shore) and for ever after the place was known as Bogn(omen)or(ae)!

More recently, in July 1978, M Kendell wrote from Coney Hill Cemetery in Gloucester (he was superintendent there) assuring us that a "simple inversion" to 'Rognob Regis' (unless an inhabitant could produce a "more inspiring idea") would be enough to persuade him to honour us with a visit. And in 1985, the *Southern Caterer* ran a competition to rename Bognor, awarding first prize in August to Mr & Mrs Walker of North Bersted, for 'Kingshaven on Sea'. In response, an *Observer* survey of local opinion came up with 'Bognor Mortis' or 'Costa Geriatrica' from taxidriver Ron Buttle, but most residents thought any change would be for the worse, and Margaret Warner, an "exile" at Abingdon, claimed that 'Bognor' retained for her a "special charisma" and an occasional weekend here was "an emotional experience".

Generally speaking, it seems, those who live here and have grown fond of the place, are content with the name; their nicknames stem from affection and are aimed at those who seek to disfigure the town or to change its image or character - 'Butlin Regis', 'Prowtingville', or 'Pensionville', for the developers of holiday camps, housing estates or rest homes, 'Bognor Rubble' for the demolishers, 'Dognor' for the defilers of clean pavements. It is outsiders, perhaps - the journalists, cartoonists, comedians - who find Bognor objectionable, or sniggery, using it as the butt of music-hall jokes, or as an ideal contrast to more romantic place names such as Barbados or Hollywood. Whether they are ridiculing Bognor the name, or Bognor the town, is not altogether clear. 'Bog' appeals to the lover of lavatory humour, or conjures up mental pictures of dank, misty swampland; above all, 'Bognor' is a hard-sounding name that sticks in the memory; and the combination of all three is lethal. Its real meaning is said to originate in Bucge, a (female) Saxon chief or landowner, and 'ora', old English for coast, shore or landing place. This suggests that logically we should be living in Bugnor Regis, which is hardly less appealing.

Bognor as a town has never decided on which type of resort it wishes to be, or clientelle it wishes to atttract, and outsiders are equally unsure. The *Daily Mail* in January 1983 informed its readers that after Esther Rantzen's triumph as Dick Whittington in Bognor pantomime, she "left the seaside with fond memories of the Kiss Me Quick and candy floss resort", but in a report of Bognor's football team's F.A. Cup victory over third division Swansea in November the following year, described it as the "genteel" resort. If Bognor Regis as a place is chosen as a target by comedians, rather than Bognor Regis as a name, does it still conjure up an impression of being regal, select and dignified; does the 'Regis' suggest exaggerated dignity; or is it simply the epitome of dull, safe and unexciting?

The addition of 'Regis' (Latin for Royal) in 1929 made things worse and focused attention on the name. Either it was an attempt to disguise the vulgar-sounding element of 'Bognor', or a little resort's presumptious bid for greater notoriety - as one writer put it, "cashing in on the King's convalescence". The result nationally was greater derision. Locally it was, and still is, either a source of pride or a matter of indifference. A correspondent in the *Bognor Regis Post* in March 1953, asserted that:

> "The addendum 'Regis' to Bognor was not desired by the man in the
> street and in consequence was ignored. As a railway guard I found
> that 99 people out of 100 travelling to Bognor Regis were going to
> 'Bognor'. Bognor is remembered as a charming seaside town, and it
> is perhaps best that it is so remembered."

'Remembered' is the operative word. In Hotham's day they called the resort 'Bognor Rocks' to make a dull place sound grand. Today, having made a "charming" place dull, 'Bognor' on the Rocks' seems more appropriate.

OH-YEZ!
WHEN BOGNOR HAD A TOWN CRIER
(Newsletter No. 13, August 1985)

It was interesting to see the return of the town crier to herald the opening of the Garden, Homes and Hobbies Exhibition at the Bognor Regis Centre in March last year.

Several references to a Bognor crier appear in the Minute Book of the Local Board of Improvement Commissioners, established by Act of Parliament in May 1822 (West Sussex Record Office UD/BR/1/1A). The entire population of the parish of South Bersted, of which Bognor was then a part, was barely 2,000, so Bognor itself could hardly have been described as a town, but in the absence of mass media to publicise the deliberations of the Board, and with widespread illiteracy, the town crier performed a necessary duty.

The crier is first mentioned on 8th July 1822, when a week's notice was given of a special meeting to elect a commissioner to replace Richard Dally, who had assumed the office of Town Clerk: 'the above was cried thro' Bognor and stuck up in ye market'. In March the following year, the crier is named as Thomas Pipson, who seems to have caused some dissatisfaction, for in August the Board directed that the Clerk 'do give notice to Thomas Pipson that he is no longer to be considered as Town Crier and cause a notice to be stuck up that the Office is vacant and that applications may be made to the Commissioners...' Who his replacement was, isn't revealed, but on 1st August 1825, we learn that Thomas Richardson was appointed Crier.

Part of his duties involved keeping the locals in order. In July 1825 for example, he was cautioning them 'against the practice of Bathing and exposing their persons on the shore'. On November 5th, 1829, the Chairman, the Rev. Edward Eedle (vicar of South Bersted) 'ordered that Mr Dally do before the Fifth of November next, cause hand bills to be circulated in Bognor cautioning all persons against making Bon Fires and letting off Squibs, Crackers and other Fireworks, and also cause the same to be cried in the same Town'.

Two years later, a temporary Board of Health was set up to forestall the arrival of cholera in the town by improving sanitation. At a meeting held in the schoolroom adjoining St. John's Chapel in the Steyne on 2nd January 1832, it was 'moved and resolved that the Commissioners do employ a Man and a Horse and Cart to go round once every fortnight to remove nuisances by taking away all filth and manure and other collections of offensive matter ....'

All this concern for hygiene meant extra work for the crier, and in February the Board 'ordered that Mr. Eedle do pay Mr. Mason (the Chichester printer) seven shillings for printing Bills as to Nuisances and to the Crier five shillings and sixpence (271/2p.) for crying special meetings and delivering notices'.

Unfortunately, the minute books of the Commissioners do not survive beyond 1835, and in those of their successors, the Local Board of Health from 1867, the crier is not mentioned. Melville's 1858 Sussex Directory and later Kelly's, however, list Henry Puddick of Bedford Street as town crier and by the 1880's he had moved to South View, No.8 High Street (between Lyon Street and Den Avenue today).

In December 1882 the *West Sussex Gazette* reported that the Clerk of the Local Board 'had ascertained that Mr. Puddick was appointed Town Crier under an Act of George IV, and that no other person was entitled to assume the duties of the office'. By then, local newspapers were being widely read and when Mr. Puddick died in June 1889 aged 78, there was, presumably, no call for a successor.

Some Memorable Personalities

WHEN RICHARD DIMBLEBY CAME DOWN OUR WAY
(Newsletter No.6, January 1982)

Devotees of the steam radio who tune into Radio 4 at tea-time on Sundays, will be familiar with the signature tune 'Horseguards, Whitehall' and the format of 'Down Your Way'. Each week a different town or village is visited and local residents are interviewed about their community and are asked to choose a piece of music. On the 9th August 1981, the programme celebrated its 1,500th edition.

When 'Down Your Way' was first broadcast to a post-war ration-book Britain in 1946, it introduced something revolutionary to radio – the unrehearsed interview of the 'ordinary man in the street'. Portable tape recorders hadn't yet appeared and the programmes were recorded on to a blank disc in a special BBC recording car. In her article in Radio Times in August 1981, Gay Search described the foretaste of 'Beatlemania' that the 'Down Your Way' team provided, when the listening audience was ten times the present one million. "It was a little like a royal progress, with the police needed to clear the streets for the recording car, the local press out in force and crowds of peoples waiting to see Richard Dimbleby, even to touch his coat for luck".

While recently looking through some back-numbers of the 'Bognor Regis Post' I came across a 'preview' they had given, on the day before Richard Dimbleby's familiar voice introduced 'Down Your Way' from Bognor Regis, on Sunday 14th September 1947. "We never look under any carpets. We only try to find nice things and nice people," claims Brian Johnston, the present interviewer. I doubt if the police were needed to control the crowds in sleepy Bognor, but here from the newspaper report, are the nice people who spoke on 'Down You Way' at Bognor Regis.

It was 11.30 on a warm but overcast Wednesday morning, when the BBC team, including Mr John Shuter (producer), Mr Richard M. Lane (engineer) and Mr G.D. Marvin (programme assistant), drew up on the Esplanade opposite the Pier, headed by Mr Howard Cotterell, the town's publicity officer, who had prepared the ground, "The engineer ruefully draws the attention of the 'Post' reporter to the dilapidated condition of the mudguards. '...but we can always say that the public might not like it if we drove up in a Rolls Royce."

Mr Dimbleby, "tall, plump, witty and jovial," arrives and soon puts everyone at ease. He introduced Bognor Regis with a mention of King George's recuperation here 18 years earlier, before proceeding to the first 'port of call', the Red Cross Centre in Waterloo Square, where he spoke to the commandant Miss K. Davidson, of 'Bascombe', Chichester Road. "And how many cases have you treated roughly during the past year?" he asked a Red Cross helper. – 1285 since Whitsuntide. Miss Davidson's choice of music was Stravinsky's 'Fire Bird Suite'.

- 69 -

Next was Mr E. M. Jones (Ted Jones', added the 'Post'), physical training and sports organiser for the Bognor Council, who tells of the children's sports to be held on the sands later in the day and selects Tchaikovsky's 'Romeo and Juliet' overture.

Down on the shore, Mr Billy Welfare, local fisherman, related how he had served as a coastguard, in the Army and Navy, and how two of his daughters were now in Canada. Appropriately, Vera Lynn sang "We'll meet again".

After luncheon at the Rock Gardens and a few words with the receptionist, Miss Paula Cleveland, about her passion for horses (choice of music not revealed) the team proceeded to the library in London Road – it was tucked away out of sight in a hall behind Hansford's the outfitters, - where the Head Librarian, Miss D. F. Musk of 12 Canada Grove, presumably revealed to the nation Bognor's reading habits before settling for Chopin's 'Fantasy Impromptu'.

Mr A. E. Tout, newsagent at Webster & Webb's stationers at 61-65 High Street, enthused on the lure of picture postcards. Mr Dimbleby had noticed at the railway station that morning the brisk trade in postcards, despite the exorbitant price of 5d plus 2d for postage. Choice of music – Handel's 'Largo'.

At Bognor Riding School in Upper Bognor Road (presumably at the corner of Mead Lane?), Mr H. Rose maintained that four lessons were sufficient for the most awkward novice to learn how to sit on a horse and extolled the joys of riding on the sands, adding effect with the 'Post Horn Gallop'.

On to No. 23 Sandymount Avenue, where Bognor's younger generation was represented by Miss Jean McKinley, who said how much she enjoyed Westloats School (one of the finest in the South of England) and the delights of bathing at Bognor in the summer. "Any record from Rawicz and Landauer" – no punk rock in those days.

Out in the country at Chessels Farm, Flansham, Mr Owen Adames assured Mr Dimbleby that farming was 'no job for idlers' before relaxing 'In a Monastery Garden'

In those days the programme ran for an hour, but time was nearly up as the team made its way to the opposite end of the town to interview Mr & Mrs E. S. Densley at 'Brownie' Barrack Lane, Aldwick. Both fresh out of the R.A.F., they were busy building a T.V. set (Ah, the novelty of it all! "We never did complete it" Mr Densely tells me).

Tchaikovsky again – this time 'Serenade for Strings' – before the programme ended at King's Drive, Pagham, where Mr Dimbleby's son David was staying. "But we will let David speak for himself on Sunday", said the 'Post' tantalisingly. I wrote to Mr David Dimbleby, asking him if he possibly remembered his stay in Bognor and he very kindly replied: "I remember either I or my mother had fallen off a horse, I cannot remember which, and this seemed to be the main part of the interview. We had a great discussion in the family about what I should call my father, whether Daddy, Sir or Father. I think we ended up, in a very old fashioned way, with me calling him Sir. I was asked to choose the request record and plumped for 'Men of Harlech' which was the only title I knew."

I thought it might be a good idea to obtain a tape of the programme for one of our meetings, so I also wrote to B.B.C. Sound Archives. Sadly, they searched in vain for the recording. It was only possible to keep a small fraction of their vast Broadcasting output and 'Down Your Way' was poorly represented in the Archives, they said. Alas, a gem of social history lost forever! Just as well the 'Post' gave us a good run-down on it.

Sources: Bognor Regis Post, 13th September 1947 page 1 &
                       20th September 1947 page 3
      Radio Times 8th-14th August 1981 pp 6-8.

....

W. P. MARSH – ARTIST WITH A CAMERA
(Newsletter No.11, July 1984)

Collectors of guide books and early postcard views of Bognor will be familiar with the name of W. P. Marsh, local photographer of the late Victorian and Edwardian period, whose "Marvellous Instantaneous Photographs of high seas and breaking waves" were to prove extremely popular as souvenirs of the resort, and win him recognition both nationally and abroad.

William Pankhurst Marsh was born at 26 York Street in Dover, on October 9th 1850, the son of William Marsh, a victualler, and Charlotte, nee Sinclair. His fascination with the sea in all its moods were probably inspired by watching the waves pounding the shoreline of his home town, and it may have been here that he learned his trade – the 1858 directory of Dover lists one 'photographic artist', Josiah Ferdab.

It was in 1875 that he opened his studio in Waterloo Square Bognor, behind the Beach Hotel in premises now [2004] occupied by an ice-cream and cold drinks outlet. He had married an Ashford girl and in the 1881 census the family were living at Norfolk Cottage in Norfolk Street, behind the studio. The census also reveals that their first child, then six year old, was born at Chichester, which suggests that they lived or stayed there for a short time before moving to Bognor.

By the 1890s his reputation had spread. Two of his seascapes were featured in 'The Ocean of Air; Meteorology for Beginners' by Agnes Giberne, published in 1891. In April 1893, Marsh exhibited at the National Photographic Exhibition at the Crystal Palace:

"Several of the London daily and other papers of last week have spoken highly of Mr Marsh's work. Last Friday evening a collection of lantern slides by Mr Marsh, most of them scenes along the coast at Bognor, were thrown upon the large screen in the theatre at the Palace before a large audience, a special bi-unial optical lantern being used, and judging by the applause which greeted each picture (especially those of the 'High Breaker' and 'Prawn Fishermen Ashore and Afloat') the Bognor views were highly appreciated."

To cater for the growing popularity of picture postcards around the turn of the century, seaside photographers generally were widening their 'repertoire' of subjects to include street scenes, local events and celebrities. Marsh's portraits of Bognor fishermen and the renowned bathing woman Mary Wheatland were an example, among them a rare glimpse of her in everyday clothes rather than her heavy serge bathing apparel.

Four studies of rough seas at Bognor and Aldwick appeared in 'The Picture Magazine', Vol. 3 January - June 1894, with reference to "the unrivalled collection of Mr W. P. Marsh of Bognor, who has been awarded for his phenomenal skill in obtaining these majestic pictures many prize medals, including that of the Royal Photographic Society". Included was his most famous –

a view from the Pier of high seas hitting the sea wall at the foot of Lennox Street and captioned: "Giant Breakers at Bognor ... Several of Mr Marsh's studies have been enlarged in carbons up to 48ins x 36ins.. When thus first shown in a London shop window, such large crowds collected that, in consequence of the obstruction caused, the police made a complaint."

One of these enlargements, framed and behind glass, hangs in the entrance foyer of Bognor Regis Town Hall today, but close proximity to the rent and rates offices may render it less of a crowd-puller.

The 'Practical Photographer' proclaimed in 1897: "Bognor is noted for its seascape photographs. During stormy weather, Mr Marsh is always out on the promenade or pier. Often the wind is too strong for a tripod to be used, and the camera is placed on the floor of the pier, to be held down by a firm hand while he releases the shutter..." High seas at Bognor in those days were more spectacular and frequently caused flooding in York Road and Belmont Street. This was remedied in 1914 when the sea wall was strengthened by curving the top outwards with a 'bullnose' of concrete, thereby deflecting the impact of the waves.

Marsh's advertisements boasted proudly of patronage by Queen Victoria and the Prince of Wales, later Edward Vll, and hence his studio was named the 'Royal Marine Studio'. His price list included the following 'hints to sitters'-
'...with the perfected arrangements for lighting which have been adopted at this Studio, any day except very dark cloudy or stormy ones will do--.
Come early in the day, and never when in a hurry or fatigued. The expression cannot be satisfactory when the Sitter is wearied or anxious about time, etc...
Large Checks, Plaids, and conspicuous Stripes are not favourable to the artistic treatment of a picture...
Children's Portraits are the most successful in light colours, as dark dresses increase the length of exposure...
It is not always expedient to follow the fashionable mode of dressing the hair, as it is sometimes very unbecoming.
When in the Studio try not to be anxious as to the result. The photographer will do his best for his own reputation. If not, no amount of anxiety on your part will enable him to do his work any better. *Above all, don't bring all your friends to see you photographed.'*

Clearly, having your photograph taken in Victorian days could be a harrowing experience for all concerned. Mr Marsh was also emphatic that credit was to be 'in no way solicited or entertained – Only Terms: Cash when the Order is booked'.

The Marsh family later made their home on the opposite side of Waterloo Square at No. 13, which he named 'Marina'. Around 1905 he moved both home and business to No. 39 Southgate, Chichester (now a second-hand bookshop) where he died on March 18th 1918 and was buried in Chichester Cemetery. His obituary in the Bognor Observer spoke of his 'quiet and unassuming disposition' and his 'calm and considered judgement' while serving as a member of the Bognor Council for ten years and as Chairman of the pier Committee. He left a widow, Margaret Jane, who lived to the ripe old age of 96 years in1947, and two daughters: Georgina, who married a Lionel Price Evans, and Blanche, who became Mrs Despard.

The death two years earlier from illness of his only son and partner in the Chichester business, William Lindsley Marsh, must have been a great blow to the family. He was 31 years old, had been a keen footballer, a 'capable' rink skater, a member of the 'C' squadron of the Sussex Yeomanry, and was popular at local concerts as a 'Scotch humorist' and impersonator.

William Marsh senior, though, had ensured that his name would live on. His Bognor successor, Donald Massey was already by 1910 inviting prospective customers to inspect his latest breaking-wave pictures at his London Road studio. But W. P. Marsh was the pioneer, and the products of his artistic skill not only helped to spread the fame of Bognor far and wide, but a century later provide good quality illustrative material for local historians. Many of his photographs form part of the Seymour Collection and will be a valuable contribution to our museum exhibitions.

William Pankhurst Marsh, 1850-1918.

FOOTNOTE
I was intrigued by W. P. Marsh's second Christian name, but both Marsh and Pankhurst were fairly common surnames n the 1851 Census of Dover (two of these, William B. Marsh and Cullen Marsh were proprietors of Bathing Establishments) and it is unlikely that he was closely related to the husband of the famous Suffragette, Richard Marsden Pankhurst, who was born in Manchester in 1836. By coincidence though, Marsh's daughter Blanche married a Herbert Patrick Despard – at one tine the joint Secretary of the Women's Social and Political Union (formed by Emmeline Pankhurst in 1903) was a Mrs Charlotte Despard.

Sources: 1851 Census of Dover (PRO ref.HO107/1632,f.352, p.18)
Birth Certificate of William Pankhurst Marsh.
Correspondence with the County Library, Dover
1881 Census of Bognor (PRO ref.RG11/1124, f.51, p.2)
Bognor Observer, 19th April 1893 (Crystal Palace Show)
2nd September 1896 (Advertisement)
1st December 1915 (Obituary, W.L. Marsh)
21st March 1918 (Obituary W.P. Marsh)
Gravestone inscription, Chichester Cemetery.
Information on photographs featured in publications, is from the Gerard Young Collection, W.S.R.O., and from his column in the Bognor Regis Post, 23/1/65.

....

ERIC COATES LIVED HERE
(Newsletter No. 16, February 1987)
Last summer, B.B.C. Radio 2 broadcast a 4 – part series, 'Eric Coates, King of Light Music', to commemorate the centenary of the composer – conductor's birth on August 27th. Composer of numerous suites, marches, ballets, rhapsodies and songs of universal appeal, Coates's first orchestral success was his 'Miniature Suite' in 1911, but it was the B.B.C.'s selection of his compositions as signature tunes which brought him wider recognition. Among these was his most famous, the 'Knightsbridge March' (used for 'In Town Tonight' from 1933 and to open the Sunday television service in 1950s); 'Calling All Workers' ('Music While You Work'); 'By the Sleepy Lagoon' ('Desert Island Discs'); and the 'Dambusters March'.

London was more conducive to composing and convenient for his professional commitments, but Eric Coates also needed the "soft, fresh air of Sussex". From 1922 he and his wife, Phyllis, and son, Austin, lived at various locations in Selsey and Sidlesham, before moving to 'The Holdynge', a house in Aldwick Avenue, Bognor Regis.

In his autobiography, 'Suite in Four Movements' (Heinemann, 1953), Eric Coates writes affectionately of Selsey: "...this unpretentious village, with its bathing, its glorious beaches, and its life-giving air, which three features, are beyond the powers of man to despoil". He describes the delights of the omnibus ride to Chichester, or ("most perilous journey") by the "antiquated" Selsey Tramway.

Summer explorations led them one day to Pagham Harbour –
"a lonely spot on the other side of the Point, where the sea at high tides laughed at the puny efforts of man-made defences and invaded what was once upon a time green pasture-land. At the side of the swirling waters, warmed by the sun, was a quiet pool, and here Austin would play with the tiny crabs..."
Thereafter, many happy 'cove days' were spent here.

I wondered if there was a special reason for deserting Selsey for Bognor Regis, and was Pagham Lagoon, on the Bognor side of Pagham Harbour, a possible source of inspiration for 'By the Sleepy Lagoon'? I wrote to Mr Austin Coates, and he very kindly replied.

The seaside homes were not for holidays; they were "non-London homes" which offered cleaner air. Direct exposure to Selsey's sea air, though, aggravated his father's asthma and he needed to be closer to medical help. Paradoxically, his parents both felt better for being near the sea, so Bognor was chosen rather than Chichester. A doctor friend had stipulated a row of trees as shelter from the sea air and 'The Holdynge' proved ideal, being situated on the north side of Aldwick Avenue. In April 1952 the 'Bognor Regis Post' columnist, Morton Swinburne, informed readers of Eric Coates' arrival at Aldwick, trusting "that our town and its surrounding will provide a source of inspiration."

The personal charm of Eric Coates was as well known as that of his music. After his death in the Royal West Sussex Hospital on December 21st 1957, Mr Swinburne again, recalled the personal help and encouragement he had given to the local Operatic Society as their President, attending all the final performances where possible and sitting near the conductor. Some committee members once asked him for his signature – he responded by jotting down some bars from 'Knightsbridge'. One of our members describes the composer as a "gentle gentleman". He recalls the occasional telephone call from London when a weekend at Bognor was planned, and a delivery of vegetables, meat from Parfrement's and bread from King's the bakers was hastily arranged!

Of his parents, Mr Austin Coates says "they both of them loved their years in Bognor and felt a great attachment to the place." Replying to my 'Lagoon' question, he says
"About our 'cove' days on the East Beach at Selsey, yes, the cove was in the Pagham direction, but I don't think we ever got quite as far as Pagham Lagoon. Even to get to

'our' cove took an awfully long time on those terrible pebbles. It was, however, that view looking over to Bognor which inspired 'By the Sleepy Lagoon'."

This point, he says, is mentioned in an introduction by Ian Lace to a 1986 re-issue of Coates's autobiography 'Suite in Four Movements' (Thames Publishing, £14.95).

Recommended is Geoffrey Self's biography 'In Town Tonight', from the same publisher to mark the composer's centenary (£6.50).

ERIC COATES

"THE DREAMIEST WEE TOWN ON THE SOUTH COAST" A CARAVANNER'S VIEW OF BOGNOR 101 YEARS AGO

(Newsletter No.27, August 1992)

If you have ever spent a holiday in a modern caravan, or dreamed of a carefree life of horse-drawn travel on the open road, then spare a thought for Dr. William Gordon Stables, M.D., C.M., R.N., the pioneer in the 1880s of caravanning for pleasure – the first "gentleman gipsy" at a time when the working population had very little opportunity for travel other than an annual day trip by rail to the seaside.

Dr. Stables was born in Banffshire, Scotland, in 1840, the son of a vintner, and educated at Aberdeen University. During nine years as a Royal Navy surgeon and two years in the Merchant Service, he travelled the world before settling at Twyford in Berkshire around 1875. Here, he adopted the name Gordon Stables, and his past experiences, his medical and scientific knowledge and love of nature inspired some

150 books and countless articles and treatises on a host of subjects. These included numerous adventure books for boys, full of stirring incidents and bravado in far-off lands; in 1899 he was elected most popular contributor to "Boy's Own Paper". He was a member of the Humanitarian League and Wandering Secretary to the Sea Birds Protection Society. He married, in 1874, Theresa Elizabeth Williams, who bore him four sons and two daughters.

Dr. Stables envied the freedom of gipsy life and in his mid-forties decided to adopt their mode of travelling the countryside. The traditional gipsy "vardo" wasn't good enough for a gentleman's needs, so he commissioned the Bristol Wagon Company to build him a horse-drawn van to his own design; it resembled a Pullman railway carriage and he named it "The Wanderer". Details of it construction and an account of his first major expedition from Twyford to Inverness along roads as yet unpolluted by a single motor-car, are related in his book "The Cruise of the Land Yacht Wanderer", published in 1886. It was the first of many journeys, accompanied by an ostler, two mares, his Newfoundland dog named Hurricane Bob, Polly the cockatoo, his valet (Arthur Foley, who rode ahead of the entourage on a tricycle and camped in his own tent), occasionally his children, but never, so it is said, his wife.

In 1891 this remarkable character discovered Bognor. The local "Observer" in August that year carried an interview with the doctor, who had set up camp in a field belonging to Dr. Alfred Conder on the Felpham Road at Upper Bognor. His new book on caravan life "Leaves from the Log of a Gentleman Gipsy" was all but complete. In the preface he says:-
"I am writing these lines on 24th August 1891, in my camp at Bognor, by the sea. Bognor is the quietest, cosiest, cleanest, dreamiest wee town on the south coast ... I cannot help saying that my holiday at Bognor has been one of the most refreshing and restful any man could enjoy."

In September 1891 two more columns penned by the doctor appeared in the "Observer" – one ("A leaf from the Log of a Wanderer") being an essay on caravan life in general, and the other entitled "Bognor as a Health Resort", praising the charms of a select and peaceful little town of a century ago, was reprinted from the "Bazaar, Exchange & Mart" of 2nd September 1891. At a Bognor Local Board meeting on 2nd October the Clerk was instructed to send a letter of thanks to the doctor for his interest in the town and for publicising it in the London and local press.

Dr. Stables later contributed a weekly "Health and Home" column to the "Bognor Observer" from October 1902 to June 1909, in which he advised on such diverse subjects as diet, dyspepsia, clothing, the care of children, infatuation in love and (August 1904) the "shameless" and "shocking" sight of teenage girls paddling in the sea with raised dresses!

Unfortunately, this advocate of the early morning cold-water bath was also over-fond of a "wee dram" or two; this, and an earlier addiction to chloral, contributed to his death on 10th May 1910 at Twyford, three years after becoming the first vice-president of the newly formed Caravan Club. His caravan is preserved at Bristol Industrial Museum.

The 'Wanderer's' camp at Bognor, October 1891
(From a photograph by W.P. Marsh; W.S.R.O. F/PD.50)

Sources   Gordon Stables: The Cruise of the Land Yacht "Wanderer" Hodder & Stoughton 1886 (first pub. in "Leisure Hour" 1885/6 and republished by Kylin Press Ltd. Waddesdon, Bucks 1984)
Gordon Stables: Leaves from the Log of a Gentleman Gipsy (Jarrold & Sons 1891)
Alan Stanley: "The Age-old Lure of the Open Road" in Yesterday in Hampshire, Sussex and Isle of Wight No. 31, November 1990, pp 8-9
Nerissa Wilson: Gypsies and Gentlemen (Columbus Books, 1986)
Dictionary of National Biography
Who Was Who, 1897-1916
The Times, 12th May 1910 (obituary), 13th May 1910 (death & funeral)
Bognor Observer, 1891: 26th August, p.4; 9th Sept, p.8: 16th Sept p.8
West Sussex Record Office, UD/BR/1/8, p.145, Minutes of Bognor Local Board – 2nd October 1891

"THE BOGNOR WALTZ"

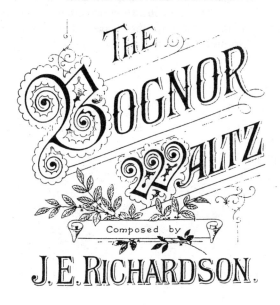

Composed by

J. E. RICHARDSON.

Copyright — Price 1/- net.

London:
Cary & Co.
Oxford Circus Avenue, 231, Oxford Street. W.
Publishers of THE IDEAL PIANOFORTE SCHOOL.

THE MAN WHO COMPOSED THE "BOGNOR WALTZ"
(Newsletter No. 28, February 1993)

A couple of years ago, the society gratefully received from a member, Mr Maurice Beckingham of Bedford Avenue, some sheet music entitled "The Bognor Waltz" composed by J. E. Richardson and published by Cary & Co. of London. This once belonged to Mr Charles Hemingfield, organist at South Bersted Church for 53 years and headmaster of the church school there for 38 years, before his death in 1950. So far, I have uncovered the following brief details about the composer.

John Elliott Richardson, son of John Richardson, grocer of Winchester Street Salisbury, was born at Salisbury 24th July 1825. He was still living there, and already a Professor of Music, when he married Sarah Clarke, daughter of John Clarke, deceased, at St Pancras Church in London on 25th June 1849.

He apparently arrived in Bognor in the 1880s. Kelly's Sussex trade directory of 1887 is the first to list him at No 4 Argyle Terrace, and at No. 10 in 1890. He later moved to No. 3 St. George's Villas in Sudley Road, where he was described as Teacher of Music, and by 1899 was established at Clayton House, No. 41 Lyon Street*.

"THE BOGNOR WALTZ."

Mr Richardson died on 22nd September 1903, aged 77, and was buried in the Roman Catholic cemetery in the grounds of the Servite Convent, Hawthorn Road (his wife had died four years earlier, aged 82). The "Bognor Observer" obituary spoke of his "kindly manners and gentle courtesy" of the former appearances of "our old and respected Chief of Orchestra" at the Assembly Rooms, and that prior to his conversion to Catholicism he had "filled with credit" the distinguished position of organist of Salisbury Cathedral. Eve May, our Chairman, [now Secretary] tells me that the Bognor Waltz is rather strident – more like a march!

Sources not mentioned
1891 Census return for Bognor, ref.RG.12/842, folio 101
Marriage Register of St. Pancras Old Church, London Metropolitan
Archives. My thanks to Mrs R. Ritchie of Selsey, for checking the entry
*No. 41 Lyon Street was later the home for 30 years of Frederick William Masters, described at his death in January 1962 as "the last of the Sussex Rusticware potters" Mr Masters, who destroyed the formula for his work, learnt his craft at Rye. The museum there received several examples of his work.

....

THE ROSSETTIS AT ALDWICK
(Newsletter No.32, February 1995)

Mention of the Pre-Raphaelite movement may bring to mind the poet and painter, Dante Gabriel Rossetti. But most of us know less of the sister whose life he overshadowed, even though Christina Georgina Rossetti has been described as 'probably the major woman poet of Victorian Britain'. Many of us will be familiar with her haunting carols, 'In the bleak mid-winter' and 'Love came down at Christmas'. At a local level, Dante Gabriel's visit in 1875 has been recorded on one of Arun District Council's current rash of royal-blue plaques, commemorating notable residents and visitors to the area; but not a lot of people know that Christina came too. As December 1994 was the centenary of her death, at the age of 64, this seems an appropriate time to remind ourselves.

Rossetti's plaque has recently been placed on a brick gate-post in Belmont Street, just east of the Arcade – a tempting target for vandalism, but perhaps the firm of solicitors who occupy Belmont Lodge were none too pleased at the prospect of visitors tramping up their gravel path to read an inscription on their private garage.

Aldwick Lodge, pulled down before the 1914-18 war.

This single-storey building was formerly a coach-house which Dante Gabriel Rossetti used as a temporary studio by kind permission of a fellow artist, William S. Burton, who lived at Belmont Lodge. Rossetti was staying at the time (October 1875 until early July 1876) at Aldwick Lodge, possibly on the recommendation of another artist friend, James Smetham, who was familiar with Aldwick. Unfortunately, the stay coincided with a particularly bad spell of wet and windy weather, the house was partly shaded by tall trees and the windows were 'hooded'; this affected the lighting quality, hence the Bognor alternative.

Aldwick Lodge was a late-Georgian house which stood in secluded grounds behind the high wall on the west side of Dark Lane. It was demolished before the First World War, when Aldwick Grange was built to the south-west. An 'Egyptian' style fireplace from the large bow-windowed drawing-room, which Rossetti used as a studio, was one of the features preserved at the Grange. Rossetti arrived plagued by insomnia, drug addiction and persecution mania, in retreat from a writ and unpaid bills in London. Nowadays, the weekly planning applications suggest that the felling or official mutilation of tall trees is a regular local pastime; but when a storm toppled an elm on the lawn of Aldwick Lodge, and the cows were feeding on its branches, he interpreted this as an ill-omen, using it in a sonnet 'The Trees of the Garden' (he had witnessed similar occurrences at his Chelsea home and at Kelmscott, in Gloucestershire). (1) He took 'violent' walks along the beach, east and west, 'among the ruined wooden groynes which had become sea-weed gardens, hideous of aspect, as if invented and laid out by fish made man'. (2) On December 3rd that year it snowed. Despite distractions, he painted industriously and among his sitters were his much-loved Janey, the wife of William Morris (who modelled at Aldwick for his 'Venus Astarte') and Alexa Wilding ('The Blessed Damozel'). Several other friends came and went, including George Hake and his brother, Rossetti's physician. And for Christmas, his sister, Christina and their mother and aunts, arrived.

On 19th January 1876, he wrote to his mother: 'I often think of the extremely happy time we passed at Christmas here, and of your good health and good spirits at the time'. Christmas Day, though, 'was a disappointment. Four ladies faced four gentlemen grimly across the table', and Rossetti said 'it looked as if I was going to preach a funeral sermon. The food got cold and the cook could not make puddings'. (3)

To many who have encountered the work of the enigmatic Christina Rossetti, she is the 'archetypal melancholy Victorian spinster'. Her childhood was a happy one but following a crisis in adolescence, her life was dogged by ill-health, by the restraints of poverty, her family, society's attitude to women and above all, by a deep devotion to High Church religion which contributed to at least two unhappy love affairs, to repressed emotions and an inner loneliness. She was born in December and died far from peacefully in another December, not before the tragic deaths of all her relatives bar one, and most of her dearest friends, including, on her 53rd birthday, the man she loved the most.

It is hardly surprising therefore, that so much of her prolific output is preoccupied with the darker side of life. Even lighter material such as the following lines from 'The Prince's Progress' touches on the frailty of life:
"Life is sweet, love is sweet, use today while you may;
Love is sweet and tomorrow may fail:
Love is sweet, use to-day
But there is also the joyful 'My heart is like a singing bird ...' (from 'A Birthday') and her many delightful children's poems, including the intriguing best-known 'Goblin Market'; or the expressive simplicity of 'The Wind':
Who has seen the wind?

Neither I nor you:
But when the leaves hang trembling
The wind is passing thro'.

Or again, we have the teasing 'Winter; My Secret', which displays the same question and answer technique and begins:

I tell my secret? No indeed, not I:
Perhaps some day, who knows?
But not today; it froze and blows and snows,
And you're too curious: fie!
You want to hear it? Well:
Only, my secret's mine, and I won't tell.

'I wear my mask for warmth', she confesses in a later line. In real life she did just that.

In a cutting on Christmas carols from the 'West Sussex Gazette' in December 1991, I read that Christina Rossetti wrote 'Mid-winter' in Bognor. Could this be another local claim to fame? Alas, no – unless she visited Bognor earlier in her life. 'Christmas Carol' as it was originally entitled, was published by Macmillan in the first collected edition of her work 'Goblin Market, the Prince's Progress and Other Poems', at the end of 1875, around the time she visited her brother at Aldwick. It was one of thirty-seven poems previously published in periodicals (4) and this particular one was written in the 1860s. (5) Gustav Holst, the composer, (whose ashes lie in Chichester Cathedral) set the lines to music early this century. Because she and her family destroyed many of her personal papers, it would require painstaking research to discover whether she wrote anything during her brief Christmas stay.

A stone was said to mark the site of Aldwick Lodge in the 1960s (6) since when the new housing development of Lodge Close has materialised close-by and recently I was unable to find any such stone – maybe someone can help. If not, is this another blue plaque candidate?

Sources: (1). Gerard Young 'A Troubled Mind in Bognor' in the Bognor Regis Post 28th August 1965 & 'Rossetti at Aldwick', 3rd December 1966. Georgina Battiscombe, 'Christina Rossetti' (Constable 1981) pp.156-7.

(2). Lindsay Fleming, 'The History of Pagham in Sussex' 1949 Vol. II p639, Quoting from W.M. Rossetti, 'Dante Gabriel Rossetti, his family letters with a Memoir', Vol. II pp319-332 & 337.

(3). Frances Thomas, 'Christina Rossetti' (The Self Publishing Association Ltd., Hanley Swan, Worcs., 1992) esp. p.306.

(4). Kathleen Jones, 'Learning not to be first; The Life of Christina Rossetti' (The Windrush Press, Glos., 1991), p.127.

(5). Joanne Shattock, 'The Oxford Guide to British Women Writers' OUP1993, p.370.

(6). Gerard Young, op.cit., 1966.
See also: Jim Allaway, 'How Rossetti Gained Inspiration at Bognor', in the Bognor
Regis Observer, 12th July 1974

....

LAURIE LEE STAYED HERE
(Newsletter No.37, September 1997)

'The stooping figure of my mother, waist-deep in the grass and caught there like a
piece of sheep's wool, was the last I saw of my country home as I left it to discover
the world.'

So ran the opening lines of 'As I Walked Out One Midsummer Morning', the
second volume of autobiography by Laurie Lee, poet and writer who died on 13th May
1997. The volume, 'Cider With Rosie' (1959), told of his village childhood in the
Slad valley in Gloucestershire. Shortly before his 20th birthday following four years
office-work in Stroud, he set off to walk to London with 'a small rolled-up tent, a
violin in a blanket, a change of clothes and a tin of treacle biscuits ... in a pair of thick
boots and with a hazel stick in my hand.'

The year was 1934, and he was able, unhurriedly, to savour the sights and sounds
and scents of freedom on unscathed country roads. 'No one could make that journey
today' (he was writing in the 1960s) ... the motor car, since then, has begun to cut the
landscape to pieces, through which the hunched-up traveller races at gutter height,
seeing less than a dog in a ditch.'

He had never before seen the sea, so his journey was a round-about one via the
Wiltshire Downs to Southampton, where his first attempts at busking proved
lucrative. A few miles on he reached the briny: 'it was green, and heaved gently like
the skin of a frog, and carried drowsy little ships like flies.' Captivated by this new
marine experience with '... the sight of the quick summer storms sliding in front of
the water like sheets of dirty glass' he pushed on into Sussex:

> 'The South Coast, even so, was not what I'd been led to expect –
> from reading Hardy and Jeffrey Farnol – for already it had begun to
> develop that shabby shoreline suburbia which was part of the
> whimsical rot of the Thirties. Here were the sea-shanty towns,
> sprawled like a rubbishy tidemark, the scattered litter of land and
> ocean – miles of tea-shacks and bungalows, apparently built out of
> wreckage, and called 'Spindrift' or 'Sprite O' The Waves'. Here
> and there, bearded men sat on broken verandahs painting water-
> colours of boats and sunsets, while big women with dogs, all
> glistening with teeth, policed parcels of private sand. I liked the

seedy disorder of this melancholy coast, unvisited as yet by prosperity, and looking as though everything about it had been thrown together by the winds, and might at any moment be blown away again

I spent a week by the sea, slowly edging towards the east, sleeping on the shore and working the towns. I remember it as a blur of summer indolent and vague, broken occasionally by some odd encounter. At Gosport I performed at a barrack-room concert in return for a ration of army beef. In front of Chichester Cathedral I played 'Bless this House', and was moved on at once by the police. At Bognor Regis I camped out on the sands where I met a fluid young girl of sixteen, who hugged me steadily throughout one long hot day with only a gym-slip on her sea-wet body. At Littlehampton, I'd just collected about eighteen pence when I was moved on again by the police. 'Not here. Try Worthing' the officer said. I did so, and was amply rewarded.

Worthing at that time was a kind of Cheltenham-on-Sea, full of rich, pearl-chokered invalids. Each afternoon they came out in their high-wheeled chairs and were pushed round the park by hired men. Standing at the gate of the park, in the main stream of these ladies I played a selection of spiritual airs, and in little over an hour collected thirty-eight shillings – which was more than a farm-labourer earned in a week. Worthing was an end to that chapter, a junction in the journey, and as far along the coast as I wished to go. It was the third week in June, and the landscape was frosty with pollen and still coated with elder-blossom. The wide-open Downs, the sheep-nibbled grass, the beech hangers on the edge of the valleys, the smell of chalk, purple orchids, blue butterflies and thistles recalled the Cotswolds I'd so carelessly left. Indeed Chanctonbury Ring, where I slept that night, could have been any of the beacons round Painswick or Haresfield; yet I felt further from home, by the very familiarity of my surroundings, than I ever did later in a foreign country.'

In Putney he sought out Cleo, a 'heart-stoppingly voluptuous' girl-friend he had met in Stroud. But her father and ideology were all she had time for, so he took a room over a cafe where he consumed meat pies and tea 'so strong you could trot a mouse on it', then moved again; labouring all the while on a building site and scribbling lines of poetry. After a year he sailed to Vigo in Spain, travelling on to Toro and Madrid. Another year on, the beginning of Civil War led to evacuation by Royal Navy destroyer. Back home again though, he had second thoughts, and in the autumn of 1936 crossed France and the Pyrenees to join (disinterestedly) 'The Cause' – but that's another story, told in 'A Moment of War' (1991).

After such adventures, his one-day encounter with the scantily-clad girl on Bognor sands would have lain low in Laurie Lee's memory, but maybe it had something to do with his return here, in 1940. Gerard Young related the story in his weekly column in the 'Bognor Regis Post' in 1969, when 'As I Walked Out...' was about to be published.

War-time regulations had deprived him of his caravan home at Storrington, so he moved along the coast again, with his knapsack, arriving at Bognor in 1941. A flat advertised at No. 17 Waterloo Square (the one with the Chinese style balcony next to the RAFA Club) was taken, so he settled for a cottage behind, in Market Street.

Casual work for the local Council paid initially for the weekly rent of 10 shillings. He stayed for nearly two years, on an off, between trips to London (working from the GPO and Crown Film Units) and home to Stroud. On such occasions he would post the rent with a letter to Mrs Savage, his Bognor landlady, and her daughter, Audrey. Mr Young's article included quotes from the letters, which continued after Lee left in 1943 to live in London (he became Publications Editor for the Ministry of Information). They were appreciative of 'the true salt smack of Bognor air', or of his room which 'looked sweet with its flowers and all. I do thank you for making it so nice. It's a garret fit to starve in now.' Audrey, who worked as a land girl at Wittering, lived at Waterloo Square as Mrs Sutherland into the mid-1970s – I wonder whether she, or the letters, survive today?

Predictably, the cottage is no longer there – it had gone 'recently' in 1969 and the rest of Market Street followed suit in 1970s. The photograph above is one I unwittingly took a year before, looking south towards the back of the Royal Hotel – Laurie Lee's cottage was the white-painted one, left foreground.

The first poem he saw printed, was one he 'dashed off with a sixpenny postal order' to the 'Sunday Referee' at Putney in 1935, but some of his earliest published poems were tapped out on a typewriter at his seaside 'base' in Market Street. And as a boy living across the street at No. 8, Martin Briggs is alleged to have been chased by Mr Lee after kicking a football through his window pane – where are you now Mr Briggs?

In his latter years at Slad, Laurie Lee was 'amiably secretive', scorning telephones and entertaining only friends within his clematis-clad 'bolt-hole'. 'There's one great thing about modern living' he told Philip Oakes of the 'Sunday Times' in 1969, 'the faster you travel, the less welcome you are when you arrive.' His writing was never fast, re-writing and 'boiling it down all the time' – the process took four years with 'Cider With Rosie', six years and one year fallow with 'As I Walked Out...'. The poems, sketches and essays were models of 'quality before quantity' and all the more welcome when they emerged. But their popularity stemmed from more than mere nostalgia for the idyllic elements of a vanished rural world. 'The astonishment and pleasure at what I began to discover around me had continued almost undiminished' he wrote in his preface to 'I Can't Stay Long' (1975): he possessed not only a deep love of nature and an incredible eye for detail – but also the gift to convey the same to his readers. As John Ezard expressed in his 'Guardian' tribute, 'he had a nightingale inside him, a capacity for sensuous lyrical precision rare in writers ten times more grandiose'.

So, the next time you encounter a busker in the local shopping centre – remember Laurie Lee with his violin on Bognor sands in the 1930s, and be not too disapproving!

Sources: Laurie Lee, 'As I Walked Out one Midsummer Morning (Andre Deutch, 1969).
Philip Oakes, 'Down to the Bare Bones' in the 'Sunday Times 1st June 1969.
Gerard Young, 'A Poet in Market Street' in The Bognor Regis Post' 20th September 1969.
Alan Franks, 'Living by the Book (Slad Valley preservation battle) in "Sunday Times Magazine' 29th July 1995.
Various national newspaper obituaries, May 1997

A POSTCARD ROMANCE IN 1909
(Newsletter No. 44, February 2001)

In his talk on picture postcards in November 1999, Steve Harris drew our attention to how the scribbled messages on the back of the cards offered glimpses into social history. A small bundle of sixteen postcards in my own collection are a good example of this.

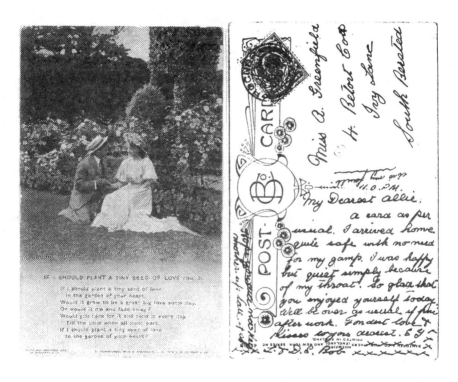

I cannot recall where or when I acquired this bundle, although it must have been before 1980, because I quoted from one of them in a half-page of postcard messages in our very first newsletter of August 1979. All but two of the cards illustrate popular hymns and songs of the early 1900s (e.g. Lead Kindly light, Eileen Alannah, If I should Plant a Tiny Seed of Love). For the deltiologists among us, they were published by Bamforth & Co. of Holmfirth near Huddersfield. The firm was founded in the 1870s and progressed in 1902 from lantern slides to postcards, noted for artistic song and hymn cards, comic and patriotic cards, etc..

But the real interest lies in the romantic missives scrawled on the back mostly in pencil by 'Bob' to Alice, alias Miss A. Greenfield of 4 Retort Cottages (now No. 13 Ivy Lane) at South Bersted. All sixteen cards bear the halfpenny stamp franked with 'Bognor' and with various dates from 4th October to 15th December 1909. On nearly every other morning, it seems, Bob posted a card to Alice, commenting on the evening before and promising another visit later that day – one was postmarked 3.45 pm – and presumably delivered the same afternoon. This was, after all, when the telephone was in its infancy, never mind e-mails (Bognor's first exchange opened seven years earlier).

Bob's messages often touched on the weather, Alice's health, or his own health, but sometimes other matters too:

Oct. 13th: "My dearest Allie. Just a note hoping you are still feeling well, & that it did not upset you last night my skylarking. Will be over tonight as arranged. Isn't it rotten weather again. Never mind it is all in one's lifetime, chop chop. Fondest love and kisses to you dearest, Yours ever Bob."

Oct. 21st: "… Hope you are feeling well this morning as it leaves me with the Merry W.W. (liar). A beautiful fine day at last. Hope you did not feel miserable last night after I left. The time with you in the front room was the most pleasant time I have spent to a certain extent. Fondest Love & Kisses to you my xxxx dearest from Y L. & D S. Bob xx"

Oct. 26th:"… I will go tonight as it is wet to my club if you don't mind. I made a world record of running last night. I got home in 4 minutes from the time I left you till I reached home…"

Nov. 11th: "… I hear Mr Dadswell got off yesterday which no doubt everyone will be pleased to hear…"

Nov. 17th: "… Mother Dad & Dot are going to see the skating this evening, so if you would care to go I will take you. F L & K to you dearest from your F L & D S, XXX Bob"

Dec. 10th: "My Dearest Allie, Hope you will like this set [of cards] & also that you will not forget yourself, when we are saying goodnight. Isn't it wet again. Fred has not come this morning as he cannot see out of his eye. F L & K. D. E Y L & D S. Bob xxxxxx"

Heady stuff indeed! But how far did Bob have to run to get home in 4 minutes on October 26th? A little research revealed that Alice married Robert Andrew Charles Blake at South Bersted 3 ½ years later on 22nd June 1913. Alice was then aged 27, the daughter of Thomas William Greenfield, a labourer; and Bob, aged 23, was the shop-assistant son of William Charles Blake, a Coastguard Pensioner at Felpham. Following the footpath from Ivy Lane, over the railway (no concrete footbridge in 1909), to the Felpham rife bridge and beyond, Bob must have been the first ever 4 – minute miler!

Ivy Lane South Bersted. Nos 1-7 Retort Cottages were the terrace on the left (reputedly so named because they were faced with material lining the inside of the old gas retort in Shripney Road). Alice Greenfield in 1909 lived at no. 4, now no. 13 Ivy Lane.

Using directories and electoral and parish registers, it is possible to sketch the progress of Bob and Alice. They set up home first at No. 14 Coastguard Cottages in Felpham. When their son Robert Victor, was baptised at South Bersted in 1915, Robert senior was described as 'worker in Aero Engines' – perhaps he was employed by the Norman Thompson seaplane factory at Middleton. Geoffrey was born eight years later. The family moved twenty years later to 'Bramleigh' in Flansham Lane, and by 1939 to 'Coburg' No. 38 Linden Road in Bognor, a house previously occupied by members of the Greenfield family.

Sadly, Bob died age 61 in 1952, but Alice lived on for another 25 years, and it was probably soon after his death that the treasured bundle of postcards were disposed of and came into my possession. But was this just a small portion of a much larger collection?

Alice and Bob in later life.
Photographs kindly donated by their daughter.

Robert junior died in 1987, leaving Emma and June Blake residing at Linden Road in the voting register for a couple of years. I wonder if they are still around. If so, I hope they'll forgive this intrusion into the once private mail of one of their ancestors.

WHO WAS 'UNCLE GEORGE'?
(Newsletter No.50, March 2004)

'Uncle George Edgar' in his 29th season at Bognor's sands (1925)
(W.S.R.O. GY PH.419).

In the history of seaside entertainment, concert parties bridged the divide between the 'nigger' minstrels and pierrot groups of the Victorian era, and the indoor summer shows of the mid 1900s. Every Edwardian resort had its concert party favourites, and anyone familiar with Bognor before it became Bognor Regis, would have seen 'Uncle George' and his troupe performing on the sands in the summer months.

'Uncle George Edgar' was the stage name of Augustus Gage Alfred Sears, born in Marylebone in 1864, the son of Emma and Alfred Sears, a builder from Buckinghamshire. In his twenties, Augustus gave up his job as office clerk in a London business house (where he sang in his firm's concerts) to become a comic on Margate Pier. He must have been popular from the start – his former employers kept in touch, topping up his funds for the next 40 years.
After seven years at Margate he was drawn to Bognor. That was in 1897, and from his Paddington home he returned each summer for 30 more seasons. Often he claimed that he had had first refusal of the site occupied from 1900 by the Olympian Gardens concert party enclosure at the foot of Lennox Street, and it may have been such an offer that first drew him here.

Initially, he brought with him his troupe of artistes known at 'The Thespians', dressed in green blazers and straw hats, and down on the sands opposite the Steyne they would perform dramatic sketches and recite comic songs, accompanied by Uncle George on his portable harmonium "squash-box". "He was," said his obituary in 1928, "a really good turn in his younger days, his speciality being descriptive songs which he rendered with dramatic gesture and telling effect. He was also a keen student of Dickens and his portrayal of characters from the famous author's novels was a distinctive feature of his repertoire."

"The children loved him" recalled Mrs Brimacombe in her description of Bognor at the turn of the century (Newsletter No. 2, 1980). She remembered his "jolly red face", winning a sixpenny workbox covered with shells as a prize, and hearing 'Uncle Harry', who assisted Uncle George, sing 'On Coronation Day' around the time of Edward VII's coronation in 1902.

Referring to seaside shows in 1900: 'The End of an Era' (1960s), John Montgomery wrote of the Thespians:
"… the troupe included Gus Davis from the Moore and Burgess minstrels, Charles Crannit (ventriloquist), Fred Warwick (versatile comedian) and Harry Everett (pianist). Their humour was topical; their songs were catchy; the audience joined in. Maybe they were not great stars, but in their time they were good family entertainers… [they] performed twice daily during the summer on the sands and West Parade and also at the Pier Hotel in the evening after 9pm. A children's singing competition was held, a fresh song being taught each week."

Among other Thespians over the years were Harry Sturgeon, W. Gilligan the pianist, and Butt (Albert Charles) Norton, a humorous vocalist from Marylebone, who loved Bognor and was laid to rest in the cemetery here in 1960.
The act did not always fit cosily with Bognor's then sedate image. Veteran seaside entertainer Clarkson Rose in May 1966 recalled Uncle George's fondness for drink which kindly elderly ladies would try to reform. If he espied their approach, he would switch his harmonium rendering from 'I do like to be beside the seaside' to 'Abide with me'!

Send-off benefits were arranged by friends before his end-of-season returns to London – similarly, (so an ex-Bognorian and ex-London policeman once told Gerard Young), a pub near his local police station in London, would 'see him off' to the seaside the following spring!

'Uncle George' became a local institution, often joined by other visiting artistes and in hard times (wet weather, for instance) was helped out by Bognor locals. And in turn, he didn't hesitate to help fellow strugglers. He was known affectionately as 'Old Bars' from his well-known monologue 'Bars of Iron'. In time his troupe disbanded and he continued as a solo act with his accordion near the Beach Hotel, employing a young boy named Brooks to collect money in a hat. Eric Hughes of Bognor later recalled him rather sadly as '"a broken-down, red faced man with a rather leering smile, playing his harmonium hopefully."

Rheumatism and heart trouble took their toll. On Boxing Day, 1927, aged 63, he died in his sleep at his home at 23 Woodfield Road, Paddington (the house is now gone) and was buried in an unmarked grave (no.12276 section 3T), in Paddington Old Cemetery, Willesden Lane.

But that wasn't quite the end of his Bognor act. In Noel Coward's 'Cavalcade', opening in Drury Lane in 1931, the Brighton seaside scene was based on The Thespians at Bognor. In childhood Coward had performed in Uncle George's show a quarter of a century earlier. Born in Teddington in 1899 and moving to Sutton in 1905, he recalled the event in his autobiography, 'Present Indicative', first published by Heinemann in 1937:
"We went to the seaside every summer for a fortnight, Broadstairs or Brighton, or Bognor. It was at Bognor that I met Uncle George's Concert Party. I shall always remember Uncle George and his 'Merrie Men' with tenderness. They held for me a romantic attraction in their straw hats, coloured blazers and grubby white flannel trousers. They had a small wooden stage on the sands on which they performed every afternoon and evening. Uncle George himself was the comedian and Uncle Bob, I think, was the serious vocalist. I forget the names of the others excepting Uncle Jack, who was very jaunty and sang, 'Put a little bit away for a rainy day,' swaggering up and down the stage and jingling coins in his trouser pocket.
Uncle George gave a song-and-dance competition every week for the 'Kiddies', for which I entered my name. I don't think Mother was keen on the idea, but she gave in when she saw how eager I was. On the evening of the competition I put on my sailor suit and waited in a sort of pen with several other aspirants, noting with satisfaction that those who appeared before me were inept and clumsy. When my turn came I sang, 'Come along with me to the Zoo, dear', and 'Liza Ann' from The Orchid. I also danced violently. The applause was highly gratifying, and even Mother forgot her distaste of Uncle George's vulgarity somewhat and permitted herself to bridle. At the end of the performance Uncle George made a speech and presented me with the first prize, a large box of chocolates, which, when opened in our lodging, proved to be three parts shavings."

On 6th April 1907, at St. Stephen's Church, Hammersmith, Uncle George had married 18 year-old Lilian Loving Earwaker, otherwise Gladys Groth, the adopted daughter of Dr Lorentz Albert Groth, a Swedish civil engineer. Uncle George's death, 20 years later, was registered by his own daughter, Edna. I wonder if she married and whether any descendants of Bognor's popular entertainer of 80 years ago are still around.

One of Uncle George's audiences.
Vanessa Mills: Bognor Regis: - A Pictorial History (Phillimore 1995)

Sources: Obituary in Bognor Post 7th Jan. 1928: Gerard Young 'The Beach Entertainers' in Bognor Regis Post 2nd June 1961: W.S.R.O., Gerard Young Collection notes, file GY5004/2B/U.I: 1881 Census (PRO ref RG.11/0156. folio. 66: RG11/0686. f.56): 1901 Census (RG.13/2552. f.24): GRO copy of marriage & death certificates: Information from Alperton Cemetery Office, Wembley.

"UNCLE" GEORGE'S BENEFIT CONCERT

(From the *Bognor Observer*, Wednesday 31st August 1921)

'On Thursday evening last, "Uncle" George held his benefit concert on the Pier alfresco stage. A large audience was present and thoroughly enjoyed the entertainment provided, the principal item of which was the children's singing competition for prizes, given by "Mr Answers", local friends and Visitors.

The first prize winner was Miss Edna Scott, a very talented artiste, who was encored for excellent songs: second prize winner, Miss Elsie Booker, and third prize, Miss Gracie Brooks. First prize for boys, Master Frank Cox; second prize Master Billy Thurston. Miss Peggy Thurston and Vera Shelly were given consolation prizes. Other artistes who appeared were Mr Jim Sheppard, Mr Butt Norton, Miss Violet Bale, "Uncle" George, the veteran entertainer in songs and monologues, and the Misses Scott (Nellie, Ivy and Edna), whose singing, duets and dancing "brought down the house." These talented young ladies are the daughters of Mr Bill Scott, of London, the well-known bookmaker of Tattersells. Mr Fred Shepherd gave his cornet solos in his usual brilliant manner, and thanks are due to Miss Maisie Hyde whose pianoforte solo and accompaniments were greatly and deservedly appreciated. Thanks are also due to Mr Phil Harriss, of London, who kindly judged the singing competition, and whose tact and affability brought a pleasing contest to a successful issue. The National Anthem concluded a most pleasant evening.'

Bricks and Mortar

REMEMBERING DR. OSBORN.
(Newsletter No.15, August 1986)

Minus its tap and downgraded today as a receptacle for litter, the drinking fountain featured on our cover was erected 100 years ago outside the Bedford Hotel (now 'The Unicorn.') by the local Friendly Societies in memory of Dr.Charles Osborn, who had attended to their members' needs. (A horse trough also stood here until its removal to Hotham Park Children's Zoo in 1966)

'The oldest member of the medical profession in Bognor' was how the *West Sussex Gazette* described Dr.Osborn, following his death on Boxing Day,1885, aged 75. Born at Littlehampton, he settled in Bognor at Frederick Place, High Street - a terrace largely replaced by Barclays Bank in 1969 - and was listed as 'chemist and medical student' in the 1851 Census. He was later Medical Officer of Health to the Westhampnett Poor Law Union and to the Bognor Local Board, whose Minute Book in Nov.1884 records a salary of £52.10s p.a.. His son, Dr. Frank C.Osborn succeeded him as M.O.

The Bognor and Bersted Friendly Society - an early form of Assurance Society dispensing benefits to the poor for sickness and death - was founded at a meeting held 25th June 1832 and chaired by Bersted's vicar, the Rev.Eedle. The Earl of Arran was its first President and capital was raised initially by donations from wealthy local residents like him.

From 1836 the scheme, originally for females and children only, was extended to males and to neighbouring parishes. There were five classes of contributions in 1884; Class I ranged from 3 1/2d (1 1/2p.) per month at age 15 to 1s 0 1/2d (5p) at age 50, assuring a weekly sum of 2 shillings during sickness, £2 on death. In Class V these rates were multiplied five times. (From the Society's handbook, Gerard Young Collection.)

WILLIAM HARDWICKE AND THE 'SUSSEX HOTEL'
(Newsletter No.18, January 1988.)

Sudden name changes, like the disappearance of familiar land-marks, are not always easy to accept, and 'The William Hardwicke' sounds a bit of a mouthful for a local hostelry known simply as 'The Sussex' for so long. Nevertheless, along with their attempt to create a new image and an 'atmosphere of informal sophistication' within, the owners deserve some credit for enhancing the exterior of one of Bognor's period buildings with a fresh coat of gleaming white paint, and for preserving a link with the past by commemorating the man who built it some 170 years ago.

William Hardwicke was born on 7th May,1780 in the village of King's Caple, Herefordshire.(1) He moved to Bognor in 1806. (2), where he entered into partnership with his uncle, Robert Turner, whose eldest son was the godson of Sir Richard Hotham. In his will dated 9th June, 1809, (3) Turner stated that he had 'lately covenanted with my Nephew William Hardwicke to enter into the Brewery Business and began to build a Brewhouse Cellar, etc.' After Robert's death in November of that year, his two sons, Richard William and Nathaniel, took over the running of the brewery, situated behind Spencer Terrace in what became known as Brewery Lane - now Mead Lane.

On 16th April 1812, William Hardwicke married his cousin, Sarah Turner, (Robert's eldest daughter) by licence at South Bersted, with Daniel Wonham, an executor of Robert's will, as witness. Daniel and his son, William Kimber Wonham, were local builders and William Kimber was later to marry William Hardwicke's niece, Eliza (4) - Bognor in these early days of its development appears to have been a closely-knit community.

It was around 1816 (5) that Hardwicke built the town's first coaching inn, alongside what was then little more than a country lane, with views across open meadows to the sea. On Thomas King's 1817 map of Bognor, it appears as the 'New Inn' - a rival to the resort's first Hotel which Hotham had established at the foot of West Street. John Ewens and Richard Berry were two innkeepers in the 1820s. Pigot's directory of 1832 listed Mary Hewlins as the proprietor and informed stage-coach travellers that the 'Comet' departed from the New Inn 'daily in summer, and every Monday, Wednesday and Friday in winter' for its 9-hour journey to London. The inn was also a meeting place for the Local Board of Commissioners, set up in 1822 to run the town's affairs - aided, no doubt, by the occasional alcoholic tipple!

The Sussex Hotel with (left) Camden House, William Hardwicke's home, demolished 1930's

Hardwicke, who owned several chunks of land in the parish built coach houses behind the New Inn and, further back, a long malt-house - this disappeared only recently, along with Lumley & Hunt's former premises in London Road. Next-door to the inn he built Camden House, a 3-storey residence where he and Sarah raised a family; tragically though, their two daughters both died in December 1824 - Ann aged 8 and Fanny aged 2 - and their only son, William Robert, a B.A. graduate of Trinity College, Cambridge, and Associate of King's College, London, died aged 26 in 1856.

William Hardwicke senior departed from the local scene on 2nd May,1865, and beneath a report of the opening of Bognor's new pier two days later, the West Sussex Gazette paid the following tribute to him:

'This week we depart from our usual custom of simply recording the death in our obituary column, by noticing more particularly in this place the decease of Mr.William Hardwicke, who died at his residence, Camden House, on the 2nd inst. . ... In this gentleman we trace, perhaps, nearly the last link that connected us with bygone days ... In early life Mr.Hardwicke proved himself to be clear sighted and energetic, and amid great activity found time to devote to subjects of public interest. He was one of the first elected to serve as a commissioner of the town, and died its oldest member. In such a position it was not to be expected that he gained the approbation of all, consequently his firmness met with opposition because the feeling was at times mistaken. Time, however, proved that in judgement he was seldom wrong, and this led many to seek his advice upon subjects of private interest, which he always gave with great kindness and courtesy. For the last few years he had relinquished all things pertaining to that of a public nature, feeling that gradual decline of life, he patiently awaited the end of it, and then with Christian fortitude worthy of imitation, resigned it ...' (6)

William Hardwicke's grave at South Bersted is visible from the pavement close to the School House in Bersted Street.

From his will - an interesting though tedious 12-page document - we learn that he had at least two brothers and three sisters, all by then deceased but having provided him with a fair number of nephews and nieces. Amongst the extensive real estate, mention is made of 'the freehold Public Houses called 'The St..George & Dragon', 'The Black Bear', 'The Ball's Hut', and the copyhold Public House called ' The New Inn', (now the 'Labour- in -Vain') situated respectively in Felpham, Pagham, Walberton and Westergate', which he bequeathed to Richard and Nathaniel Turner on payment of £3,000. His widow's inheritance included a legacy of £500, Camden House and the Sussex Hotel. along with 'my wearing apparel and watches and my wines, liquors and articles of domestic consumption and all my household goods and furniture, pictures, prints and books, plate, linen, china and other household implements and effects.'

The New Inn was rechristened the 'Sussex Hotel' (it was listed as such in the 1851 census). In 1855 Algernon Bramwell had moved across the High Street from the York Inn, replacing Henry Holman Wood as 'livery stable keeper, job master and fly proprietor,' as well as acting as agent for the Scottish Provincial Fire & Life Insurance Company. After his death a year or so later his widow, Caroline, and daughter Alice Mary, ran the hotel until the 1890's. Another daughter, Elizabeth , became the first bride to be wed at St.John's Church in the Steyne, when she married John Naldrett of the Norfolk Hotel in June 1873.

From 'Visitor's Guide to Bognor & its vicinity' pub. by J.Osborn, High St. Bognor. 1839.

The 'Sussex' became a rendezvous for local clubs and societies, among them the Bognor Cycling Club, re-formed in 1895. It was in 1898 (7) that the simple Regency facade was extended on the west side in a more pub-like style with florid Victorian decorations. Bed & Breakfast at the hotel in 1906 cost 4 shillings (20p) a night single, 6s. double, or full board for 63s, (£3.15) per week. (8)

The garden of Camden House next door was the venue for Sunday School treats around the turn of the century, until Staley's store and adjacent shops in London Road were built in 1913. The house itself provided (as its neighbour had once done) a temporary town hall while the present one in Clarence Road was under construction in 1929. Camden House was replaced in the mid 1930's by an extension to Staley's - later Bobby's, and recently 'Seasons' - closed 2004

Sources:-

(1) 1851 Census of South Bersted (HO 107/1653) fo.473, p.13..
West Sx. Record Office, MP 1882-4; Memorial Inscriptions. South Bersted.
(2) Statuary declaration by William Hardwicke, dated 8th Nov. 1853, in writer's possession.
(3) W.S.R.O. STA 1/13, p198.
(4) William Hardwicke's will, 7th July 1864, obtained from Somerset House.
(5) Bognor Regis Post, 4th April 1959. p.12.
(6) West Sussex Gazette, 11th May, 1865. p.3.
(7) Bognor Regis Post. 4th April, 1959, p.12.
(8) Ward.Lock & Co. Guide to Bognor, 1905-6.

....

THE HOUSE THAT GHANDI VISITED.

Another bit of Bognor that bites the dust..
(Newsletter No.20, January 1989)

'The design distinction and quality of an
area leaves a lasting impression on tourists,
and affects local peoples' views and use of
an area. The importance of style and design
should not be under-estimated.'

These heart-warming words appeared (according to a local newspaper) in a report produced in November 1987 by Arun Council's Director of Planning, Mr.Ian Sumnall. Was this, perhaps, some belated recognition that Bognor Regis may still be worth visiting for its historical assocations and for the remains of its architectural heritage - rather than South Coast World, Rainbow's End and candy-floss? The report was in fact recommending that redevelopment of the eastern side of Waterloo Square should adopt a style which reflected Bognor's Victorian past. I suppose pseudo-Bognor could well prove to be a crowd-puller, but how shameful that more concern isn't shown for the genuine article, which redevelopment elsewhere in the town continues to destroy.

A stone's throw from Butlin's multi-coloured shanty-town (good 'lasting impression'?) there survived until recently a residential area south of High Street, with a pleasing variety of late-Victorian and Edwardian houses. Almost unnoticed, demolition in January and February 1988 removed two fine examples in Campbell Road - the 'Dutch House' and 'The Lawn', the latter associated with the revered Indian leader, Mahatma Gandhi, who paid a brief visit here one hot October day in 1931.

A large area both north and south of this eastern end of High Street, was once owned by Claude Bowes-Lyon, 13th Earl of Strathmore and grandfather of the Queen Mother. He purchased Sudley Villa, west of Sudley Lodge, in 1863, nicknaming it 'The Den' (Lyon Street, Glamis Street and Den Avenue commemorate him). The seaboard portion of the Strathmore estate, bounded by Clarence Road and Gloucester Road and protected by covenants against trade or business development, remained open meadows until the 1890s.

The West Sussex Record Office holds building plans for houses on both sides of Campbell Road, submitted by William Tate (see page 26, newsletter No.18) who, by mid 1895, had completed Bognor's eastern promenade and sea-wall. The 'Dutch House' was the first in this road. approved by the Urban District Council on 6th September 1895 for Mrs.Emily Ward, who had established the Norland Institute for nursery nurses in London three years earlier. (In 1907 she was to open a holiday home for nursery children at 4 Field Row, Gloucester Road and another for trainee nurses and children at Field House, on the corner of the Esplanade, in 1910. Notable guests included the late Princess Marina of Kent and her two sisters, and in 1938, the two children of the German Ambassador, Ribbbentrop.) With its Dutch gable, (fashionable in Bognor around this period) and 'curb roof' providing walls half clad in blue-grey slates, half bricks and pebble-dash, the 'Dutch House' exemplified a picturesque break from Victorian formality. Messrs.Kidney & Berry, of Old Broad Street, London, were the architects.

Plans for 'The Lawn , with its half-hipped roof and generous use of flints, were approved on 16th October 1896, although the house appears to have been built closer to the road than the plans suggest. William Tate was the architect and the house is listed in local directories as 'Cothele' in 1899 and 1900, with Tate as its first resident.

By 1901 it was re-named 'The Lawn' by its owner for the next thirty years, Miss Isabella Scott.

"The Lawn," Campbell Road, (Courtesy Southdown Observer series)

Isabella Scott was born in 1835, the second of nine children of Russell Scott, a partner in Cory's coal company, and Isabella Prestwich, sister of the geologist, Sir Joseph Prestwich. Before moving to Bognor, Miss Scott had lived with her widowed mother at Norcliffe Hall, Styal, and at Broomfield, South Reddish, both near Manchester. She was a trustee of Manchester College, Oxford, and involved herself with the work of her brother, the Rev.Lawrence Scott, and the Russell Scott Memorial Schools founded by her mother, at Denton,Manchester.

Another of Miss Scott's brothers was Charles Prestwich Scott, the liberalist and renowned editor of the <u>Manchester Guardian</u> from 1872 to 1929, who had "raised a respectable but distinguished Manchester paper to a leading place as a moral force in world politics". It was on Sunday, 11th October,1911, while C.P.Scott was staying with his sister at Bognor, that Mahatma Gandhi paid a lunchtime visit. Alfred Phillips, the composer, who lived at 'Walton Walls' in Walton Road, was also present. Gandhi was attending a conference in London and had come to Chichester to spend the weekend with Bishop Bell. Those who attended the 'old films of Bognor' evening at the Regis Centre in February, 1988 may recall a glimpse of the white-robed figure emerging from the gateway of 'The Lawn'.

Mahatma Ghandi leaving "The Lawn" with C.P.Scott.

Tragedy soon befell the family. C.P.Scott died on New Year's Day 1932 at Manchester, followed shortly by his eldest son, (who had succeeded him as editor of the Manchester Guardian) in a fatal accident in the Lake District. On 21st June,1932, Isabella, the last surviving member of the family, died aged 97 at 'The Lawn' The Times obituary mentioned that for long periods she had made her last house a "delightful" seaside holiday home for poor and delicate children.

Miss Scott was buried at Marylebone Cemetery. Bequests in her will included £200 to the Commons & Footpaths Preservation Society, £200 to the Metropolitan Association for Befriending Young Servants, £500 to the Anti-Slavery and Aborigine Preservation Society, and £100 to the Wilton Street Chapel at Denton.

The next resident of 'The Lawn' was a Mrs.Muriel Wreford Lyle, of whom I have no information - perhaps a reader can help? Then in 1939, the house became St.Michael's Day School, where day pupils of St.Michael's School for girls at Upper Bognor Road could complete their schooling after the latter was evacuated because of the war. In 1945 the premises were sold and re-named St.Richard's School, teaching girls of all ages and younger boys, mainly day but with a little boarding. The Bognor

<u>Regis Observer</u> of 26th May, 1945 stressed the continuity between the two schools, with use of the same premises and staff, including the first head, Miss F J L Morley, M.A., Cantab.

Meanwhile, at the 'Dutch House' next door, the first resident to follow Mrs Ward was the Rev.Thomas Richard Grundy, M.A., a retired C. of E. minister. Among his four curacies listed in Crockford's Directory of the time, was that of Style Chapel, Wilmslow, Cheshire - in the vicinity of Miss Scott's pre-Bognor home. The Rev.Grundy moved to Bournemouth around 1906 and was replaced by Mr John Haviland, who, ten years later as 2nd Lieutenant in the Royal Fusiliers, died of wounds received in action, aged 34. The <u>Times</u> on 21st July 1916 named him as a former Northamptonshire cricketer, and a tablet in St.Wilfrid's Church records his services as churchwarden at St. John's Church and Manager of Nyewood School. The next occupants were Ludwig and Vera Ehrlich, of whom, again, I have no details. In 1950 the 'Dutch House' was linked to 'The Lawn' when it was acquired as a boarding annexe to St.Richard's School, under a new principal, Mrs.Gwendoline B Boorman, L.R.A.M., M.R.S.T.. H.M.I. Reports reveal that the number of pupils in 1946 - 103 - had fallen by about two-thirds by 1950, but later doubled (74 in 1954). The school survived until the mid - 1960's; Kelly's 1964 directory lists Reginald A Boorman as the principal.

The Dutch House during demolition, February 1988 (Photo R.Iden)

The construction of new Ministerial Offices (Gloucester House) and a telephone exchange in an empty field next door, was followed by the acquisition of the two houses in Campbell Road. 'The Lawn' was occupied for a short time by the Ministry of Agriculture, Fisheries and Food and then succeeded the 'Dutch House' as a driving test centre - to relieve Chichester's traffic problems during market days and the Goodwood season. The Bognor sub-centres closed in August 1979.

Following the usual period of wanton neglect, the last owners, British Telecom, decided there was no longer any practical use for the two premises, so yet another piece of local history and architecture, unique to Bognor, is sacrificed upon the funeral pyres of the demolition squads. In the Bognor Regis Post of 17th October 1964, Gerard Young drew attention to another curiousity at 'The Lawn' - the date '1864' spelt out (for reasons unknown) in large numerals with bottle-ends, in a garden wall which separated the house from an older property. After a brief sorte of the now empty site, I can only conclude that this has suffered the same fate as the house.

Sources.:

Dictionary of National Biography
The Times 22 June 1932; 18 August 1932.
Bognor Regis Post 25 June 1932.

Gandhis's Visit:
Bognor Regis Post 15 August 1942; 8 March 1969.

Information on St.Michael's Day School and St.Richard's School
kindly supplied by Miss Judith Lee.

Other sources:
West Sussex Records Office U.D.C. Building Plans, ref. UD/BR/16/1/998,1006.
Registers of Electors; street directories; Crockford's Directories.

Bognor Regis Post 25 October 1969, p.17.

SIR RICHARD HOTHAM'S CHAPEL.
(Newsletter No.29, August 1993)

In 1987 we celebrated, as best we could on an icy January day, the birth of Bognor as a seaside resort when, 200 years previously, Sir Richard Hotham laid the foundation stone of his first mansion, Bognor Lodge. By the end of 1792 he had completed most of the architectural legacy he was to bequeath little more than six years later, including a new residence for himself in a field next door to Bognor Lodge. This was to be known as the Chapel House (now Hotham Park House), because attached to the north-west corner, Hotham erected his very own chapel. Today the clock tower is the only part of the chapel to have survived, otherwise, on the 12th of August this year, we may well have been celebrating another stone-laying bicentenary.

In August 1788 Hotham applied to the Archbishop of Canterbury (under whose peculiar jurisdiction South Bersted and the tithing of Bognor lay) to improve the accommodation at the parish church of Bersted. Details may be found among the episcopal archives held at the West Sussex Record Office (1)

> ... the said Sir Richard Hotham hath lately purchased and
> considerably enlarged for his own Residence a Messuage or
> Dwellinghouse in Bognor within the Parish aforesaid; And ...
> hath no Pew or Seatroom within the church of the said Parish
> large enough or proper for him, his Family or Servants to
> stand sit kneel or hear divine Service in ...'

Hotham's idea was to move an existing gallery on the north side of the church 'now used chiefly by Servants promiscuously' (i.e. indiscriminately) and to replace it with 'a convenient and proper' gallery for himself and his household, complete with its own entrance, staircase and windows, and reserving the space below the staircase as a burial vault for himself. These and other improvements, totalling some £600. (2), were duly made, and at the sale of Hotham's estate in 1800, each house included a pew in the new gallery (removed during restoration of the church in 1879 - Lovett's guide book to Bognor, published soon after, recalled its 'heavy and sombre nature').

But Hotham wasn't satisfied for long - nothing short of his own place of worship, emphasising the exclusiveness of his new 'watering-place' would do. Richard Dally in his Bognor Guide of 1828 cites the distance to Bersted Church (all of half a mile!) as the reason. More likely, the growing number of distinguished visitors seeking out the little resort and cramming the pews at Bersted or Felpham each Sunday, preferred not to mix with the village yokels.. So on 12th August 1793 (neatly coinciding with celebrations of the Prince of Wales' birthday) the Duke of St.Albans was invited to lay the corner-stone of the new chapel. It was, reported the Sussex Weekly Advertiser,

> 'one of the most brilliant fetes ever known in this
> neighbourhood; every thing seemed to conspire
> to give festivity to this auspicious day: youth,
> beauty, and fashion graced this happy scene;
> the Fields of Elysium could never appear more
> transporting, nor could the influence of the
> Waters of Lethe more completely unknit the brow
> of Care - for every heart seemed to pant with joy ..
> The music consisted of twenty performers, se-
> lected from the Gloucester and Portsmouth bands,
> most of which were amateurs. The young vocal
> performer, also had a great share of merit, for to
> a sweet voice, he added taste and judgement,
> untinctured with affectation.
> Upwards of 120 persons attended .... (3)

Dr.Davis, in 1807, recalled the occasion with matching eloquence:-

> '... Sir Richard placed under the same stone a sheet of
> lead with a record of its foundation. The Duke was
> assisted upon this occasion by a numerous and
> brilliant assemblage of noble personages, gentlemen
> and ladies of the first respectability, a band of music
> preceding the open carriage in which his Grace and
> family were conducted from Hothamton Place to the
> spot.
>
> When the ceremony was performed, the band played
> "God Save the King" after which the company
> proceeded to the marquees that were purposely
> placed in the garden of the Crescent for their
> inspection. Refreshments also of various kinds
> were prepared in abundance for the party. At
> three o'clock the company assembled in the
> grand saloon, which was decorated with a
> print of the Prince of Wales, plumes of

feathers, mirrors, and branches of laurel inter-
woven with festoons of natural flowers. And here
Sir Richard evidenced his hospitality and munifi-
cence by a display of sumptuous collation,
composed of every dainty the seas afforded.

The whole concluded with a ball in the evening
at the Hotel, attended by a select party of ladies
and gentlemen; for whose further entertainment
Sir Richard had taken care to provide fireworks,
which were as advantageously seen from the
windows, as they contributed to promote, and
give a pleasing finish to the pleasures of the night.' (4)

Years passed before the chapel, dedicated to St.Alban and sometimes known as
'Hothamton Chapel' after the name Hotham gave to his resort, was used for worship.
The eight-day clock mechanism for the clock tower was dispatched to Bognor from
John Thwaites of Clerkenwell towards the end of 1794. (5) Lady Hester Newdigate,
writing home to her husband during a month's holiday in the following August,
referred to the crowded accomodation at Bersted Church:-

'Church is in ye afternoon at half past 2, but we shall
be there sooner to secure places as they say some
Ladies sat by the Door last Sunday and some could
not get in at all. It is ye smallest Church I ever saw.
Sir R.Hotham has built a very spacious chapel joyning
to his own house, but it is not quite finished and if
they are as tedious about that as about ye Warm Bath
there may be no service in it till ye Place is out of
fashion' (6)

The main stumbling block appears to have been the matter of consecration. (See
footnote, page 120) Bognor inhabitants had worshipped at Bersted Church ever since
their own chapel of St.Bartholomew had been abandoned in 1465 (7) and,
understandably, the Vicar, the Rev.Thomas Durnford, was opposed to a plan which
would rob the Bersted congregation of its newest and wealthiest members. Richard
Dally's assertion, in his Bognor Guide of 1828, that 'all difficulties were overcome' is
misleading. Despite an appeal to the Archbishop of Canterbury, a very disappointed
Hotham lost a bitter dispute with the Vicar, and had to settle for an agreement,
whereby the Rev. Archer Thompson was licensed by the Archbishop in 1797 to
officiate as Chaplain for three years.(8)

Just four years and a day after the stone-laying, the Sussex Weekly Advertiser carried a more subdued account of the opening ceremony which finally took place on Sunday, 13th August, 1797:-

'The little fashionable watering-place Bognor, is at present crowded with company of the first distinction, which gives great life and spirit to Chichester, and is of considerable service to its trade. The new chapel at Bognor was opened yesterday se'nnight by the Rev.Archer Thompson, (the celebrated Preacher at the Magdalen) who is appointed Chaplain. The subject of his sermon was the profanation of the Sabbath, on which the Reverend Preacher exerted his oratorical powers with the happiest effect. The chaste simplicity of the structure was generally admired by a very fashionable auditory. ' (9)

Only the best for Hotham! The Rev.Archer Thompson preached morning and afternoon in West London, and evenings at the 'Magdalen' a hospital in Blackfriars Road for penitent prostitutes. Combined with lecturing and charitable works, these 'unremitted professional exertions in the pulpit' led to his early death in February 1805. His father was the Rev.Seth Thompson, chaplain of Kensington Palace, who died in October the same year, only five days after christening his son's child. (10) According to Dally, Seth Thompson officiated at 'Hotham's death' in 1799. John Marsh, the composer and musician who moved to Chichester in 1787, discovered Bognor and Felpham a year later, and his diaries reveal him as a regular participator in the social and musical life of the resort until his death in 1828. (11) One entry (in August 1798) confirms that both Thompsons preached here:-

On Sunday ye 19th we went to Bognor Chapel at which
Mr.Thompson Senr. officiated whom many people preferred to
his son and at half past two drove to Felpham Church where he
officiated for Mr.Durnford.'

There are no available illustrations of the chapel. From an 1841 lithograph of the house (then known as Bersted Lodge) published by Henry Hounsom in Bognor, we catch a glimpse of the chapel's roof-line surrounding the clock tower. (12) On 12th and 13th September, 1805 John Marsh the diarist made sketches of 'Bognor Chapel', the Hotel and coffee room, Hayley's Turret House and the Crescent (Dome House etc.) but the whereabouts of these sketches is unknown.

Bersted Lodge, (now Hotham Park House) c.1841. The roof of Hotham's chapel is visible below the clock tower.

We must resort, therefore, to 'word-pictures', St.Alban's Chapel was described by Dr.Davis in 1807 as 'commodious within, and very neatly distributed, having also a boarded floor,' Sale particulars of the house and estate in 1812. (13) refer to

> 'A very elegant Chapel ... 60 ft by 42 ft. pewed all round with
> handsome Galleries over, an Altar-piece, Pulpit, and Vestry,
> painted wainscot color, and furnished in a style of chaste
> simplicity; an excellent turret Clock, and various Rooms in
> the roof.'

And according to the Visitor's Guide to Bognor and its Vicinity, published locally in 1852, over the altar were mounted 'some very valuable paintings' of the Entombment of Christ, the Descent from the Cross, and Our Saviour on the Mount of Transfiguration.

Poor old Hotham survived only a year and a half after the opening ceremony, but the chapel lived on. When the 'Hothamton' empire was auctioned in 1800, Chapel House and a lot more of Bognor was purchased by Colonel Richard Scott (who was connected with the Hon. East India Company) and soon after, sold again to Rear Admiral Sir Thomas Troubridge. During this time the chapel's first (and probably only) marriage ceremony was recorded in the South Bersted parish register, (14) On 12th September,1801, Henry Thomas Howard, of Thornbury, in Gloucestershire and Elizabeth Long, of St.Marylebone, Middlesex, were married by special licence 'in the chapel of St.Albans belonging to the Parish of Bersted', by Charles Henry Hall, Canon of Christchurch,Oxford. (The bridegroom was the younger brother of the 12th Duke of Norfolk, who later lived at Aldingbourne House and was M.P. for Arundel..)

In June 1815, Chapel House was purchased by Thomas Smith, 4th son of Sir John Smith, Esq., a London merchant, and brother of Sir John Smith Burgess, Bt. His wife was Susannah, daughter of William Mackworth-Praed, M.P. for Cornwall. Under new ownership and a new name, (Bersted Lodge), the house became the centre for lavish parties, with guests including the Duke of Clarence (later William IV) and the Earl and Countess of Mayo, who eventually became semi-permanent residents, both dying there in the 1840's. The Countess was Mrs.Smith's twin sister, Arabella, lady-in-waiting to Queen Adelaide and once unflatteringly dubbed by Lady Glengall as 'the ugliest woman in the world'.(15)

But the renaming of the house did not herald the abandonment of the chapel - rather the opposite. Those invaluable diaries of John Marsh again, record a burgeoning interest after his first meeting with the Smiths at a concert held at the resort's subscription and coffee room in mid-August 1817. Three days later:-

> Mrs.Smith and Lord Mayo, staying there, showed me the chapel
> and organ, which had 2 barrels for psalm tunes, and a spiral
> one for voluntaries, which played the Hallelujah in the
> Messiah, Dead March in Saul, and Coronation anthem, which I
> heard, and was much pleased with both the Organ and the
> Chapel, in which Mrs.Smith was so good as to show me a pew
> for Mrs.M and me to sit in the next morning .. .. On the next
> day, (Sunday ye 17th) I went with Mrs.M ... to the Chapel at
> Bognor that after having been shut up 6 or 7 years, was
> opened again for divine service this day, upon which occasion
> a Mr.Townsend read prayers and the Bishop preached and 2 of
> the Chichester choristers sang psalms .. .. in the evening
> drank tea at Mrs.Smith's, after which we went into the
> chapel to hear the organ, which played from 8 till 9.'

(Note the reference to a closure period). He was knowledgeable on church organs, supervising the fitting up of the same in the newly-built St.John's Chapel-of-Ease in the Steyne in 1821. In September 1818, Mrs.Smith invited him to meet the (un-named) 'maker of their organ, to whom I pointed out some errors on some of the barrels, that required rectifiying'. His diary lends support to Dally's statement that 'several popular ministers performed divine service to numerous fashionable auditors' at Hotham's chapel.

On 30th August 1818 Mr. and Mrs.Marsh received the sacrament when their son, Edward, preached the sermon at the invitation of a Mr.Courtney, whose own fine service at the chapel had been praised three weeks previously. In September it was a Mr.Richard, in October the next year, Mr.Atherley from Arundel ('the minister for this season') and Dr.Mant (possibly Richard Mant, the Archbishop's domestic chaplain?), twelve months later Mr.Cartwright from Earnley and a Mr.Palmer. Marsh's diary is less informative about those who came to listen; October 1820: 'Sunday 15th being a very showery day, there was a very thin congregation at the chapel.'

Thereafter, his interest appears to have waned considerably in favour of the new St.John's Chapel. This was consecrated by the Archbishop of Canterbury on 25th January 1822, and with the gradual decline in numbers of Bognor's aristocracy (compared to the heyday of 'Hothamton') may eventually have rendered the chapel at Bersted Lodge redundant. Dudley Elwes, writing in 1872, (16) says that Bersted's vicar, The Rev.Edward Eedle was 'licensed to perform the duties of the Chapel on 12th October 1841 (but which chapel.?)

The widowed Mrs.Smith died in October 1856, much lamented for her many charitable works. Sale particulars of Bersted Lodge in 1857 stated that the chapel was licensed for public worship, but not having been consecrated, might be used instead as a 'noble picture or statue gallery, or saloon.' (17) The new owner, John Ballett Fletcher, having neither sacred nor secular use for it, decided on demolition. Many a historian has reiterated 1859 as the date of this dastardly deed (and that the building had fallen into disrepair) but despite an exhaustive search of the local newspapers available for that year, and for 1863 when the perpetrator died, I can find no documentary evidence. The only clue lies in local guide-books. The Visitors Guide to Bognor and its Vicinity, published by J.Osborn in 1852 and W.Follett in 1856 (both librarians and stationers in Bognor High Street) contains a description of Bersted Lodge and St.Alban's Chapel. A 1859 edition substitutes J.B.Fletcher for Mrs.Smith and ignores the chapel. So for now, 1859 must stand (or await demolitiion)

Today, the chiming of the clock at Hotham Park House is an hourly reminder of St.Alban's Chapel - whose site is partly occupied by public lavatories. The 1857 sale particulars stated: 'from the entrance hall and attached to the residence is a private chapel ...' On the (otherwise blank) west wall at the back of the house, facing the aforementioned toilet block, is a bricked-up doorway which may have provided access to the place where Bognor's founder, and those illustrious visitors who came to see and be seen and to marvel at his enterprise beside the sea, knelt before their maker.

Sources.

(1) West Sussex Record Office: EP IV/2/28, F17 and EP IV/13/2. By permission of the County Archivist.
(2) J.B.Davis, Origin and Description of Bognor, or Hothampton, London 1807. P.87.
(3) Sussex Weekly Advertiser, 19th August 1793. P.3.
(4) Davis, Op.cit. pp 81-84.
(5) Guildhall Library Ms.6788/2, Thwaites & Reed Day Book, p.391. 31st October 1794.
(6) Lady Newdigate-Newdegate, The Cheverels of Cheverel Manor (1898), quoted in G.Young, A History of Bognor Regis, (Phillimore, 1983) p.25.
(7) Lindsay Fleming, History of Pagham in Sussex (1949), vol 1, pp 117,121; vol II, p.606.
(8) See Footnote, page 120..
(9) Sussex Weekly Advertiser, 21st August 1797, p.3.
(10) Gentlemen's Magazine, 1805, pt.1, p.191; pt 11, p.979.
(11) W.S.R.O. microfilms MF 1165-1170 (original diaries at Huntingdon Library, California, HM 54457, vols 1-37). For an extract of Bognor entries, see Dr.E.Thomas and R.Iden 'John Marsh and the Seaside' in West Susses History, No.51 April 1993, pp2-14. See also Dictionary of National Biography.
(12) W.S.R.O. PD 242, also variation in UD/BR/10/12.
(13) Gerard Young Collection, West Sussex Institute of Higher Education (ref.unknown). The sale was postponed until 1815.
(14) W.S.R.O. Par.19/1/1/5
(15) The Girlhood of Queen Victoria, vol 11, p.308, quoted in Doubleday & Lord Howard de Walden, The Complete Peerage (1932), vol VIII, p.609, ftnote b.
(16) Sussex Archaeological Collection, vol.XXV, p.121.
(17) W.R.S.O., UD/BR/10/12.

SIR RICHARD HOTHAM'S CHAPEL.
(Newsletter No.30, February 1994)

In his article under the above title, in Newsletter No.29, Ron Iden mentioned an 1872 reference to the licensing of the Rev. Edward Eedle, Vicar of South Bersted, to perform the duties of the private chapel at Bersted Lodge, (now Hotham Park House) in 1841. He has since found confirmation of this in the following newspaper accounts:-

Sussex Agricultural Express, Saturday, 16th October 1841, p.5. column a, headed 'Local Intelligence',

'BOGNOR - Fashionable Intelligence, -

'On Tuesday her Royal Highness the Duchess of Gloucester and suite arrived on a visit to Mrs.Smith, and the Earl and Countess of Mayo, at Bersted Lodge; his Royal Highness the Duke of Cambridge is expected. Divine Service will be performed on Sunday in the splendid chapel at the above mansion. The following persons of distinction continue their visit at Bersted Lodge: The Earl of Wiltshire, the Dowager Lady de Clifford, Lady Charles Somerset, Lady Cecil and Mrs.Delafield, Lady Caroline Legge, and the Hon.General Meade. Lord and Lady George Lennox are expected to return to Lennox Lodge from Boulogne in the course of a few weeks.'

Sussex Agricultural Express, Saturday 23rd October 1841 p.4 col.e.

'BOGNOR - Fashionable Intelligence.

'On Thursday se'nnight (14 Oct) His Royal Highness the Duke of Cambridge and suite arrived on a visit to Mrs.Smith, and the Earl and Countess of Mayo at Bersted Lodge. On Sunday their Royal Highnesses the Duchess of Gloucester (who had arrived a day or two before) and the Duke of Cambridge (who appeared in excellent health) attended divine service in the chapel attached to the superb mansion. The prayers were read in the most impressive manner by the Rev.J.Delafield, and an eloquent discourse was preached by our respected Vicar, the Rev..E.Eedle. The following are among the numerous calls at Bersted Lodge since their Royal Highnesses have honoured Mrs.Smith with their visit:- Gen. (continuation on page 5, col.a.) Sir George, Lady and Miss Walker; the Hon. Gen. and Mr.Meade and the Misses Meade, Mr. and Lady Sarah Bayley, Capt.Davidson, Mr.Davidson, Mrs.Edw.Nugent, Miss Julia Price, Miss Jane Price, the Rev.E.Miller, Lady Emily Ponsonby, Mr. and Mrs.Fitzpatrick, Mr.Teesdale, Rear Admiral Schoneberg (Schomberg?), etc.etc.'

Was the above a special event, and if so, what was the occasion?

Footnote:- Hotham had no wish to consecrate the chapel - the Vicar was opposed to its licensing. The dispute is the subject of an article by Ron Iden: 'Sir Richard Hotham's Chapel at Bognor' in Sussex Archeological Collections, Vol.134 (1996) pp.179-181, based on documents at Lambeth Palace Library. (See page 114)

TIME TO REMEMBER
(Newsletter No.31, August 1994.)

Question: What has been clocking up 200 years of Bognor's history and been heard by four heirs to the throne of England, not to mention generations of Bognorians and countless other visitors to Sir Richard Hotham's little enterprise by the sea?:

Answer: The clock mechanism at Hotham Park House.

Newsletter No.29 contained an article celebrating the 200th anniversary of the laying of the foundation stone of Hotham's private chapel, which was attached to his own residence, Chapel House, known today as Hotham Park House. The chapel was demolished around 1859 by a new owner of the house, but one part still survives - the clock tower - and an inscription on the repeater dial inside the tower records that the mechanism was installed by John Thwaites of Clerkenwell in 1794.

The Guildhall Library in London holds in its care a Daybook of Messrs.Thwaites and Reed, clockmakers of Clerkenwell, (ref: Guildhall Ms. 6788/2). Entry No.31 on page 391, dated 31st October 1794, is an account for the supply, packing and fixing of the clock mechanism. In 1975 I obtained a photograph of the entry and. as advised by the Library, I wrote recently to the Worshipful Company of Clockmakers, who own the archive, for permission to reproduce it here in photocopy form. Since no reply was forthcoming, I offer instead a transcript. On the original document the costings of each item were entered in letter-code; the Guildhall Library could offer no reason for the coding, but suggested a likely formula for deciphering it, and the figures quoted below are based on their formula.

	£	s	d
Sir Richard Hotham Kt.			
To a new 8 day Church Clock to strike			
the Hours on a Bell 3cwt.2qtr.3lb.8oz			
to shew 2 outside Dialls Hours & Minutes			
the Striking Great Wheel 15ins diameter			
the Watch Great Wheel 14 ins diameter			
rest in Proportion with Weights, Ropes,			
Pullies, Hands and Hammer.			
Work & every thing Compleat Except Bell			
diall Plate, Package or fixing.	66	00	0
To a new Bell wt. 3cwt.2qtr.3lb.8oz at			
16d per lb.	26.	7.	4
To 2 Copper Diall Plates of 6 foot			
diameter each with an article Moulding			
round the Edge Printed Black with Pitt			
figures & Moulding & with Proper Bolts			
& Brasses to fasten them up @ 20 each	40	00	0
To 2 Packing Cases to the above with			
Proper Package..	3.	13.	6
To a Man 12 Days fixing the above with			
Expenses of Living at Bognor and Carriage			
There & Back.	6.	6	0
Total	£142	6	10

(The actual total shown, based on the same formula, was £333.15s.0d. but this included a previous entry on the same page.)

Since then, the distinctive bell has chimed 156 times every day, or 56,940 times each year. Multiply that figure by 200, add on 48 x 156 for leap years (discounting the years 1800 and 1900) and that produces a grand total of 11,395,488 chimes - ignoring the very occasional off-periods - and the mechanism remains in excellent working order.

In volume 2 of his <u>Fifty Years' Biographical Reminiscences</u> (published in 1856), Lord William Pitt Lennox, the 4th son of the 4th Duke of Richmond, recalled a visit to Mr.Binstead's Library at Bognor, while staying at Molecombe, at Goodwood Park, in the summer of 1817, when aged 18. Here he encountered Mrs.Smith, the owner of Hotham Park House, (then known as Bersted Lodge) and her house-guest the Duke of Clarence (later William IV) and was invited to join the house-party that evening and spend the week at the house. The Duke overheard his hostess telling the young Lennox: "I premise that the only room I have vacant is rather a noisy one, near the clock", "'What's that ?' inquired the Duke; 'the clock room! - his Lordship will be sure to be called in time, which is not very usual with the young men of the present day;' and with a good humoured chuckle, he cried, 'We shall meet at dinner' ... At supper, or rather over sandwiches and negus, when the gentlemen were left alone, the same good-humour prevailed, and the clock close to my bedroom generally struck two before we retired to rest".

Other people who had good reason to remember the clock were those whose weekly task it was to wind the mechanism - usually the head gardener. This was Mr.James McFadyen from 1927, when the house and the estate were privately owned by Mr.W.H.B.Fletcher. Mr. Les Powell, who joined the gardening staff in 1929, first helped to wind the clock in 1940 and six years later, when Bognor Regis Urban District Council purchased the estate and renamed it Hotham Park, it became his official task, as a member of the Council's Parks Department. From 1966 he was assisted by a younger man, Mr. Harold Page, but in December he took along a reporter from the Bognor Regis Post:

"The measured tick of the pendulum - one swing every two
seconds - was heard by Sir Richard Hotham, 'Bognor's founder ...
The cable-suspended weights which provided the power for the
clock and the striking mechanism were not far from the ground,
they noticed as they entered the building. In a week the
weights fall nearly the height of the building.

'I have counted the rungs, but cannot remember how many there
are now,' said Mr.Powell as he began to climb the ladder. The
reporter made it 63. He found the pauses provided by the two
floors between the ground and the clock platform were
convenient places for a breather. The people who wound the
clock originally had no such pauses. They had to climb a
vertical iron-runged ladder made by setting bars into one
corner of the tower.

'Must have been quite a climb,' said Mr.Powell. He pointed
out the huge, lead-weighted pendulum enclosed in a wooden box
with a door. The wood bore dozens of names, initials and
dates, pencilled by workmen and other visitors.

To see the clock mechanism alone was worth the climb, felt the
reporter. In a cast-iron frame, rather like the ends of an
old-fashioned bedstead, were the brass cogs, looking much too
delicate to stand up to the years ...

... He fitted a handle to a square-ended shank and began winding up the clock. A large wooden drum revolved and the weight-carrying cable was slowly wound round it. He gave it 22 turns before stopping. The weight on the bell-striking mechanism is heavier and a reduction gear had to be fitted. The reporter took over and puffed through what Mr.Powell, from his experience, told him were 92 turns. Mr.James McFadyen, who ... retired about two years ago, used to wind the clock, and Mr.Powell helped him.

'We used to share winding the big one,' said Mr.Powell.

While the reporter got his breath back, he and Mr.Powell waited for the hour to strike. They admired the ingenious ratchet mechanism which 'decided' whether the bell should be struck one or twelve times. The cleverly-designed brass couplings, through which the mechanism drives the hands on the two faces outside the tower, gleamed under their coating of old grease.

Mr.Powell looked at his watch. 'Two minutes fast, I make it ,' he said. 'It generally is.' He stopped the pendulum so that the rest of the world could catch up, and a dead-looking fly on the drum stirred awake. 'Lots of flies come in here in the summer,' said Mr.Powell stopping to set the pendulum swinging again.

As they clambered down the ladders, the ticking grew fainter and disappeared. The weights were now high up in the tower. The reporter did a sum. They must have been up and down about 9,000 times since they were installed, and the clock looks good for another 9,000 weeks."

(Extracted from the Bognor Regis Post, 31st December 1966.)

When the mechanism faltered in mid-August 1971, the Post reported that repairs would be carried out by the firm that made a periodical inspection, Messrs.Smith, of Derby. I wrote in April this year to Arun District Council to enquire whether the same firm still carried out an inspection and who was currently responsible for the weekly winding. Again, I have yet to receive a reply or acknowledgement - I must be using the wrong writing-paper.

In May 1976, after years of neglect, Arun District Council applied to the Department of the Environment for permission to demolish the home of the town's founder, with the exception of the clock tower, which presumably would have been left as a monument to local apathy and philistinism. Fortunately, at the eleventh hour, a retired Buckinghamshire company director, Mr.Abraham Singer, stepped in to restore the house and convert it into private flats. When work began on the clock tower at the end of 1977, a 13 ft.antique punt gun for fowling was found in the tower. The two seven-foot diameter clock faces, fixed to the main structure by large metal bolts, were taken down. The south-facing dial had fared worse, having been more exposed to salt-laden winds from the sea for over 180 years; but the hand-beaten copper was admirably cleaned and re-enamelled and the roman figures re-gilded in gold leaf, by Mr. David Dear's local signwriting company.

Next time you are in Hotham Park, set your watch by Hotham's timepiece and take a look at the fine detail on the white-painted cupola with its colonnade of miniature Doric columns surrounding the bell - "one of the little gems of late Georgian architecture in Bognor Regis," the late Gerard Young once wrote. It matches the graceful facade of the house itself, described by Nairn and Pevsner in their Sussex volume of the "Buildings of England" series, (1965) as "the extremely prettily and elegantly detailed two-storey verandah on the east side: trellis ironwork above supported on a chaste and almost Florentine Doric loggia". The removal of the first-floor trellis, for suspect reasons during the 1977 restoration, was something I queried at the time and have regretted ever since. I hope what's left remains safe for another two centuries, as a reminder that there was once a lot more to Bognor than clowns, car parks, "caffs" and candy-floss.

UPDATE ON HOTHAM'S CLOCK
(Newsletter No.32, February 1995.)

In an article in Newsletter No.31. celebrating the centenary of the clock mechanism at Hotham Park House, I recommended readers, on their next visit to the park, to "set your watch by Hotham's timepiece'. This would have proved a little difficult since, unbeknown to me, the hands had been removed some weeks previously and the clock was silent. All was revealed in the "Bognor Regis Observer" on 27th October. At a cost of £3,000, Arun District Council had been refurbishing the tower and ending 200 years of manual winding on a weekly basis by installing an automatic winding mechanism, manufactured by the clockmakers, Smith of Derby.

Certain statistics quoted in the "Observer" suggested that someone had received a copy of the newsletter article, but had unfortunately mis-read two items: October 31st 1794 was the date of the entry in the daybook of Thwaites & Reed, the Clerkenwell firm who had supplied and installed the mechanism for Sir Richard Hotham, not the date of installation, although this no doubt took place around the same time. And, as the article pointed out, the total cost for supplying, packing and fixing in 1794 was around £142.6s.10d., not £333.15s.0d., which included another account on the same page of the daybook . (Both figures are questionable, since the original pricing is entered in code and the totals are based on an 'ad hoc' deciphering formula kindly offered by the Guildhall Library, where the document is held.) I am told that, technically speaking, the term 'chimes' applies only to clocks that play tunes. The clock at Hotham Park, therefore, 'strikes' the hours, presumably with 'strokes', as in 'at the stroke of midnight'.

The Three Rs and more

THE BOGNOR BOY'S HOME FOR WAIFS & STRAYS
1890 - 1907
(Newsletter No.34 February 1996)

(From Newsletter No.34, February 1996, following a short note on the recent demolition of the former Bognor Steam Laundry in Hawthorn Road, established by Mrs. Rhoda Verion in the 1880s)

The 25-inch Ordnance Survey map of 1898 referred only to the 'Bognor Home for Waifs and Strays' on the laundry site But the Bersted Parish Magazine of April 1890 confirmed that the laundry was already there when the Home opened:

> "On Easter Monday there will be declared open by Mrs. Fletcher, Bersted Lodge, a New Home for orphan and homeless boys. This beneficent institution has been founded by C.A. Stein, Esq. and it will inhabit the buildings next door to Mrs. Verion's well-known laundry in a part of our parish which seems to have acquired the name of New Town ... This Home is not intended for those who are entirely destitute, for a payment of about 6 shillings a week will be received on behalf of each boy from those who may have placed him in the home. Boys of 9 to 13 years of age will be taken in and clothed, fed and taught, besides the three R's, music and some useful occupation by which they may be drafted off to the Jersey Home for Working Lads, Stamford Street, London, whence situations will be found for them."

Six shillings (30 pence) a week must have been a considerable sum in 1890. Today, the building next-door to the laundry site bears a plaque 'Albion Villa 1886', and below are two shops; an Indian 'Takeaway', not long opened, and on the left Mr. Anscombe's shoe-repairing business, founded by his father in 1924. (Now in 2004, a firm of financial advisers) Mr. Anscombe told me recently, Yes, he understood from an elderly lady who lived along the road (but sadly has since died) that the building he worked in was once the Boys' Home and there was at one time more accommodation attached at the rear, including the Home's drill hall, and maybe it also occupied part of the premises later used by the laundry

Easter Monday 1890 (7th April) was described as 'a red letter day in Bognor and South Bersted' in the account of the Home's opening in the *Bognor Observer* two days later. Assembled in a 'large' room at the rear of the building were a number of Bognor's leading citizens, including Bersted's vicar, the Rev. Charles Mortlock (chaplain of the new home), Lord Walter Gordon-Lennox, the Jersey Home's Hon. Secretary (a Mr. Jones), Miss Story the treasurer, and Mr. C.A. Stein, who was involved with the Shaftsbury Home Club and Institute in London; the Bognor Home was to be affiliated with this and the nearby Jersey Home, both in Stamford Street near Blackfriars Bridge. Following a service performed by Bishop Durnford of Chichester, the home was opened by Mrs. Fletcher of Bersted Lodge (now Hotham Park House).

The proceedings then moved to the Assembly Rooms in Bognor, where the programme encompassed performances by the local band, 'humorous songs, etc.' and gymnastic exercises by lads specially brought down from London - 'neatly dressed and whose bright faces were indicative of their contentment with their lot.' Initially there were the inevitable speeches by the Bishop, by Lord Gordon-Lennox and by Mr. Stein, who each spoke of the distressing conditions of the large cities, the nature of the work of the homes and their hopes for success at Bognor. The latter told how

> "... he had been visiting Bognor during the past fourteen or fifteen years, and the reason he had selected Bognor for the locale of his home was because he was quite satisfied that there was no healthier sea-side resort in England ......
> He had heard it stated that the Home would do the town harm, and if the visits of friends from London, who were prepared to spend their money freely would do harm to the town, then he would plead guilty; but his opinion was that the Home would do the town good by causing it to be widely known. He wished to impress upon them the fact that the boys received into the Home were not of the criminal class, but were sons of widowed mothers whose only crimes were that the father had died and left them in positions not as well off as they formerly were, boys, many of whom had been tenderly reared ...."

A letter from Mr. Stein in the same issue of the *Observer* thanked those who had expressed support for the new venture. The £7.1s.21/2d (£7.06) collected at the Assembly rooms (including Lord Lennox's guinea) went a small way towards the £200 required annually, but in addition to money, 'shrubs and flowers for our garden, pictures for our walls, or books for our boy's library, together with articles of food, especially vegetables, will be gladly received.'

The response to this and other appeals, such as one in December for Christmas gifts, must have been encouraging, for on 30th March 1891, Lord Gordon-Lennox returned with other local notables to open the new drill hall extension, again reported in detail by the *Bognor Observer*. In the first nine months the number of boys was said to have risen to 33 (The census return for 1891 records 34, aged from 7 to 16 years - averaging 13 years - and originating from far and wide). The Home had now 'absorbed' two more cottages (possibly those next-door to Albion Villa?), gained half an acre of land as playing space, 'much needed' outbuildings and a garden that was cultivated and planted with trees. The superintendent and matron now had the assistance of a bandmaster, tailor and gardener. The 50ft. x 30ft. drill hall and gymnasium, with space for 300 persons plus 100 on the platform, was constructed of deal weather-boarding and iron roof and erected by Mr. F. Phipps of Bognor for around £200. Inside the hall, drills similar to those taught in the army, would be performed under the direction of Sergeant Henry Ragain, ex-Duke of Cornwall's Light Infantry; thereby "implanting into the minds of those boys the duties of life and obedience; and moreover the duties not only to their masters here, but also to their country".

This suggests a somewhat harsh regime, but the cost of the drill hall was defrayed by the musical exertions of the boys' own band at various functions in the town; and their smart dress and behaviour, Mr. Stein claimed, had already won the hearts and minds of many local inhabitants. In April 1892, for example, the Felpham Coastguards contributed to the Home the proceeds of their amateur dramatics show at the Assembly Rooms, and the response to an appeal in the *Obseerver* for gifts for the Christmas tree and help on the day resulted in a Boxing Day of 'good old English cheer', fun and feasting and 'a day of unbounded delight to the youngsters'.

But Mr. Stein's 1892 Christmas appeal was preceeded by a note of regret:

'... the friends of the particular class of children for whose benefit the Home was founded have not for some reason appreciated the efforts made on their behalf and in consequence the character of this Home has been entirely changed. We have received our certificate from the Local Government Board authorising the Boards of Guardians to send us children who would otherwise drift into the Workhouse. Although outwardly there may be little difference in the appearance of the children, yet I can assure you the majority have scarcely anyone in the world to take any interest in them and their lot is of the saddest ....'

This infers that funds were inadequate and for survival the home would have to admit children who, although no less deserving, came from backgrounds less in keeping with Mr. Stein's ideal - and probably less respectable in the eyes of some prim and proper Bognorians. The *Bognor Observer* told readers:

'We are informed that the Committee of the "Working Boys' Ladder" have disposed of this Home to the Church of England Society for providing Homes for 'Waifs and Strays', and that it will be carried on by that very large and powerful Institution as one of their Chichester Diocesan Homes on and from the 1st of January next. All outstanding liabilities will be settled by the "Working Boys' Ladder".'

To mark the change in status, the Home boys, headed by the full band under direction of bandmaster Mr. Richard Sharpe (landlord of the 'Stamp House' at North Bersted), marched to Bersted Church on New Year's Day 1893.

The Church of England Central Society for Providing Homes for Waifs and Strays had been founded in 1881 for destitute and neglected children 'by boarding them out to families, sending them to Small Homes, and promoting their emigration to the Colonies'. As such, its aims were similar to those of Dr. Barnardo (and of Mr. Fegan, whose work, inspired by an incident on Bognor beach in 1871, was chronicled in an article in our Newsletter No.23 in August 1990). The Society claimed by 1893 to have already provided homes for 3,895 children, and now had 40 homes throughout England and two in Canada.

The Bognor Home for Waifs and Strays
(Illustrated in 'Our Waifs and Strays')

Henceforth then, the Bognor Home for Orphan and Homeless Boys became known as the Home for Waifs and Strays and remained so until its disappearance from the local scene around 1907. This was the last year in which it was mentioned in Bognor Street directories and in the Chichester Diocesan Kalendar, by which time the Church of England Society's Homes now totalled 99, four of them in the Chichester Diocese catering for 44 boys at Bognor, 32 girls at Brighton, 26 boys at Burgess Hill and 6 girls at Crawley, with a convalescent home for 13 children at Hurstpierpoint. There seems to be no explanation in Diocesan and parish magazines, or local newspapers, for the Bognor Home's closure. Recently, however, the Church of England Children's Society Archives in London confirmed that they hold case files of children who attended the home (though for confidentiality, access is restricted); and that their former supporter magazine, "Our Waifs and Strays", contains references to the home. (See below)

In April 1890, 'admitted 8 boys from the Bognor Home' is the first of many references in the log-books of South Bersted village school and, after its opening in September 1990, Nyewood School. Both of these were Church of England schools and no such contingents appear to have been received at the Board School in Lyon Street. Some of the Home boys appear in a class photograph, dressed in uniforms resembling those worn decades later by devotees of Chairman Mao! With them is Mr. Edgar J. Brooke, who was master at South Bersted School from 1889 to 1897. Their irregular admissions and withdrawals, general backwardness and 'delicate' state of health on arrival, and the disruption of attendance figures whenever infectious diseases such as scarlet fever were rife, must have proved a hindrance for the master and school managers. Nevertheless, the impression is that a number of boys responded well to good teaching as well as to Bognor's healthy air, which must have been rewarding.

Sources
Bognor Observer, 9.Apr. 1890. pp. 4 & 5; 17 & 31 Dec. 1890, p.5;
   1 Apr. 1891, p.5; 20 Apr.1892, p.5; 14 Dec. 1892, p.5;
   28.Dec. 1892, pp. 4 & 5; 4 Jan.1893, p.5;
Chichester Diocesan Kalendar, 1893, 1894.
1891 Census returns, South Bersted (P.R.O. RG.12/842, ff.62-63.)
WSRO, E24/12/1 & 3 Log-books, South Bersted National School;
   E24E/12/1, Nyewood School
WSRO, Par.19/7/8 Extracts from parish magazine, 1879 - 1907
   entries April 1890 & Dec. 1892.

MORE ABOUT THE BOGNOR BOY'S HOME
(Newsletter No.35 August 1996)

A lengthy article about this home in Sheepwash Lane (Hawthorn Road), for orphan and homeless boys, appeared in the previous Newsletter (No.34). From 1890 the Home was run by the society known as "The Working-Boys Ladder" - raising boys from poverty to independence and manhood. On New Year's Day 1893, it was taken over by the Church of England Central Society for Providing Homes for Waifs and Strays, and closed in 1907.

Mr. Ralph Rayner, whose father's memories - including life as a Bognor 'Home Boy' from 1899 to 1904 - were also printed in the newsletter, has since received from the Children's Society extracts about the Home from their former supporter magazine "Our Waifs and Strays". In January 1892 they ran a feature on the "Working Boys' Ladder" and visited the Bognor Home:

> "This is a cottage home, accommodating forty little sailor laddies, who from time to time give displays of gymnastics, musical drill, rifle drill. as well as band performances - for they have a large band - singing in the gymnasium, which can seat 500 people at an entertainment .... every boy is known and is as a son to the superintendent and matron, who they call by the good old homely names of "dad" and mother .... The value of a kind home training is apparent in the respectful demeanour and the refined manner of the boys, which win them many an invitation to tea with the resident gentry."

This doesn't quite tally with Percy Rayner's experience seven years later. Probably the staff had changed, but you may recall his memory of the matron as "a harsh unfeeling, unmotherly person ... in no way suitable for the job she held. Our dining room consisted of bare walls, forms and tables, all of which had to be scrubbed by us and had to be as clean as driven snow"!

Another item about the Home (undated, but written soon after the C/E Society's take-over in 1893) described Bognor as "....probably the oldest seaside resort in the kingdom," and despite its healthy sea breezes, "still remains the old-world sleepy little town that it has been during the greater part of the century." The author had been invited to the Christmas dinner and treat: "On arrival, we were astonished at the vast amount of roast beef and plum pudding, with oranges, apples, nuts and figs, washed down by lemonade, that the average British schoolboy could stow away ..."

And in a chat with the matron and a tour of the premises,

> "... we also found out that the original Home had formerly been a builder's house, that the large workshops had been turned into schoolrooms, play-rooms, store-rooms and dormitories; that, as the number increased, two adjoining cottages had been rented, a dining hall built, and a splendid drill hall, capable of seating 300 to 400 people at an entertainment, erected .... The dormitories, each furnished with its requisite number of bedsteads, with the coloured quilts and snowy sheets, their walls covered with bright pictures and photographs of relatives, the treasured property of the boys themselves who slept in them, looked very inviting, with the sunshine streaming through the windows. The little chapel, with its Christmas decorations and organ, showed that the important duty of family daily prayer was not neglected."

The September 1903 issue of "Waifs ands Strays" launched an appeal for funds (£2,000 initially) to build a replacement Home in the Chichester Diocese. A letter from the Archdeacon of Chichester painted a picture sharply contrasting with the earlier one:

> "The work is carried on in a building which has been gradually formed by throwing together as required the houses of a small terrace. The rooms are small and inconvenient, with innumerable doors and recesses which must make the order and discipline extremely difficult to maintain."

The Vicar of South Bersted, the Rev. C.F. Mortlock, had already offered a freehold site as a gift, though evidently this wasn't accepted and four years later the Home left Bognor.

....

THE BOGNOR JUBILEE SCHOOL
(Newsletter No. 36, February 1997)

Among the many private academies, seminaries, charity schools and dame schools that existed in Bognor and Bersted in the 19th century, the earliest recorded is the Jubilee School for the education of 50 local poor girls. This was founded in 1809 by Mrs. Elizabeth Wilsonn, wife of Charles Edward Wilsonn, Receiver General for Middlesex and M.P. for Bewdley in Worcestershire who had served with Sir Richard Hotham on the Wimbledon Vestry Committee in the 1770s and who purchased Dome House when Hotham's Bognor estate was sold in August 1800.

The school was so called because it was instituted amid celebrations marking the beginning of King George III's Golden Jubilee year. On this day, a group of labourers named the 'Bognor Griners' feasted on roasted sheep and a 'plentiful sufficiency' of Turner and Hardwick's ale brewed in Brewery Lane (now Mead Lane). They had completed work on a timber 'grine' or sea defence, known as the 'Duke of Kent's Bulwark', protecting a 1200 yard frontage of land belonging to the main purchaser of the Hotham empire, Colonel Richard Scott.

Princess Charlotte, the King's grand-daughter and a summer visitor to Bognor from 1808 to 1811, was a benefactor to the school, which continued in rented accommodation until a site for a purpose-built schoolroom was found in High Street. Charles Wilsonn had purchased the site from the trustees of Robert Turner's will on 2nd August 1817 and building commenced a month later. During demolition in November 1927 (in preparation for a new bus station built in 1934) a leaden case was found, containing two George III shillings and a lead tablet bearing the following inscription: 'On the 2nd September 1817 the Rt. Honorable Earl of Arran laid the first

Foundation Stone of this Building, erected for the Jubilee School, for the education and employment of 50 poor Girls, and instituted at Bognor the 25th October 1809 being the 50th anniversary of His Majesty George the Third's Accession to the Throne'. On the reverse side: 'Patroness, Her Royal Highness Princess Charlotte of Saxe-Coburg'.

The Earl of Arran was a local resident and among some 80 invited illustrious guests, for whom Mrs. Wilsonn provided 'breakfast and cold colation' at the Dome House.

'... The Band of the Sussex Militia attended in full uniform. There were betwixt three and four hundred persons in the front of the house, on the walls, and in trees; who behaved with the utmost respect and decorum; there was not the least damage done. The company all expressed themselves much pleased; the entertainment was from one o'clock to six, with dancing on the Green.'

Former Jubilee School Building used as Council Offices c.1900

The above account, from the Hampshire Telegraph & Sussex Chronicle, also stated that the school was for 'educating, partly clothing and giving Sunday dinner, to 25 poor girls (50 once the buildings and finances allowed) ... to be brought up in the strict Principles of the Established Church of England, to make good and industrious servants'. Instruction included reading, writing and needlework. On Sundays, the Jubilee girls, in their white pinafore dresses occupied 50 gallery seats reserved for them in St. John's Chapel-of-Ease in The Steyne, where, from the 1840s, they were subjected to the fiery sermons of the Rev. Edward Miller. On 4th January 1815 the school had been accepted into union with the National Society (full title: 'The National Society for Promoting the Education of the Poor in the Principles of the Established Church') founded in 1811 with the aim of establishing a Church school in every parish. The Jubilee School was one of three 'National' schools in Bognor and Bersted, South Bersted church school being established around 1815 and an 'Infants' school in a former dispensary, at corner of Bedford Street and London Road in 1831.

Each mistress of the Jubilee School was provided with accommodation at the house - besides the large school-room, the two-storey property consisted of four bedrooms, a kitchen, scullery, coal shed and closet, with a garden in front and a large back yard. In 1823 a Mrs. Weller was receiving £30 per annum 'including firing' (a coal allowance). Later salaries were £25 per annum quoted in 1833 Education returns, £45 in 1846 and £40 in annual reports of the 1860s. The additional allowance for coal in the 1860s was £3.10s. (£3.50) and for 'Soap etc'., used in the School, £2.10s. The West Sussex Gazette on 21st January 1872 reported that Miss Mary Scovell had resigned as mistress after 30 years and would be succeeded by Miss Bowley, 'who has had management of another school in the town.' (A gravestone in Bersted churchyard records Miss Scovell's death in London on 28th July, 1877, aged 79, and claims 39 years' service at the school).

Prices of Plain Work done at the Jubilee School of Industry.

	s.	d.		s.	d.
A fine shirt, frilled, with extra work	2	0	Children's trowsers, from 6d. to	0	9
A fine frilled Shirt	1	6	Pillow cases, from 2d. to..............	0	3
A frilled ditto	1	3	Napkins, per dozen	0	9
A plain ditto........................	1	0	Towels and glass cloths, per dozen......	0	6
Ditto for a servant	0	10	A breakfast cloth	0	2
A boy's shirt from 8d. to	1	0	A fine table cloth	0	4
A shift with fancy sleeves	1	3	A coarse ditto	0	3
Ditto for a servant, no stitching	0	8	A sleeping waistcoat	0	6
Shift with hemmed sleeves, from 1s. ... to	1	3	Ditto ruffled and frilled, from 10d. to....	1	3'
Night shift, from 1s. to	1	6	Pair of pockets, from 6d. to	0	10
A cloth apron	0	4	Flannel ditto, from 6d. to.............	0	8
A checked ditto.....................	0	3	Night caps, from 4d. to	0	6
A collar and pair of wristbands	0	4	Children's petticoats, from 3d. to........	0	6
Pocket handkerchiefs, per dozen........	0	9	Frocks, from 9d to	1	0
Cambric and muslin handkerchiefs, from			A large ditto........................	1	3
1d. to	0	2	Pincloth, from 3d. to	0	6
Pair of fine sheets..	1	0	Marking letters and figures, per dozen ..	0	2
Pair of coarse ditto	0	9			

Any Article with extra work to be charged accordingly.

CHILD-BED LINEN.

	s.	d.			s.	d.
A small shirt........................	0	2	Flannel blankets from 2d. to		0	4
Bordered cap, ...	0	3	A woman's bed gown		0	9
Plain ditto, from 1d to................	0	2	Running stockings, not including materials,			
Children's bed gowns, from 2d. to	0	4	from 2d. to		0	4

Ladies are requested to send their Linen ready cut out.

Extract from the Jubilee School Annual Report, 1861

******

The survival of all these schools depended on the charity of wealthy residents and visitors, through voluntary donations and collections made during local church services. There were also small weekly payments from the children ('children's pence') and, in the case of Jubilee School, the sale of clothing produced in needlework classes and £3. 10s. in rent each year from Dr. Todd, who used part of the premises as his surgery. As early as 1810 a November sermon by the Bishop of Chichester on behalf of the 'Bognor School of Industry' (presumably the Jubilee School) raised the princely sum of £46 - today's equivalent of that amount would run into hundreds of pounds. The much-loved Princess Charlotte, who contributed towards the building costs, died in childbirth in 1817 less than two months after the stone-laying ceremony. As King Leopold of Belgium her husband continued to subscribe generously to the funds and in the early 1860s his ten guineas accounted for almost one third of the total subscriptions recorded in the annual reports.

But the wealthy aristocratic element in Bognor's population declined as the century wore on, and even the unpredictability of the English climate could have an effect; on 23rd August 1860, the West Sussex Gazette reported:

> 'The weather lately seems against all things, and the unpropitious state of it on Sunday prevented many from attending divine service and we hear the collection from this annual (Jubilee) charitable appeal fell somewhat short of the average sum usually obtained.'

After Leopold's death in December 1865, fears over the school's maintenance were reinforced when the annual church collection 'fell sadly short of the sum anticipated or required'. As a consequence, there was little room for improvements in either facilities or teaching for the children, especially in a parish containing a growing seaside resort and three elementary schools to maintain on a voluntary basis.

The 1870 Education Act sought to 'fill the gaps' in the voluntary system by prescribing a school place for every child in the country , with local elected School Boards building 'Board Schools' financed from the rates. In December 1870 an investigative committee at Bersted reported that the parish (which then included Bognor) contained at least 443 children aged 5 to 13 years, and there was suitable school accommodation for only 287. On the day of the return, only 185 were in attendance, 141 were at private schools and 117 attended no school at all. A School Board - the first in West Sussex - was formed early in 1871, a new Board School commenced in the following January, and purpose-built premises opened in Lyon Street on 1st June 1874.

This enabled the School Board to summon parents of children attending the local 'National' Schools which were now condemned as inadequate and 'inefficient'. The

Jubilee School was under fire in July 1874; attendance there was deemed to be invalid as the Board School provided accommodation for all and a 'much better education'. The Rev. Edward Eedle, Bersted's Vicar and guardian of the Church Schools for half a century, protested at the Board's interference. Apart from the fact that he had only recently spent £10 on drainage at the Jubilee School, 'the children did not want to become great scholars. There were many callings at which they might succeed without much education'.

The old 'National School' in Bersted Street closed soon after the Board School opened in Lyon Street, but the Rev. W.B. Philpot (Mr. Eedle's successor), managed to raise support for its re-opening, in August 1878. The Jubilee and Infant Schools soldiered on until the end of the decade, despite a virtual cessation of subscriptions. In the Rev. Philpot's appeal to the Board of Education for recognition of his village school at the end of 1878, he cited the Jubilee School's imminent closure as evidence of the need for facilities for those in Bognor and Bersted who still preferred a church school education for their children.

Following closure, the 'Jubilee Charity' funds were used to encourage extended school attendance of girls at both the Church and Board schools in Bersted and Bognor. Not without some protest from the clergy of both Bersted and the recently formed parish of St. John's in Bognor, the administration of the funds were eventually decided at a meeting of the trustees on 27th June 1881 (announced in the July Parish Magazine):

> '...... applying one part in the advancement of the education of girls who attend
> school, as defined by the Education Act, and who are residents in the parish
> of South Bersted, either in payments not exceeding £2 each, in order to encour-
> age the continuance of their education at school after passing a satisfactory
> examination and possessing a certificate of good conduct from their teacher; or
> in payment of exhibitions of £5 each per annum for three years, for higher
> education, or as pupil teachers.'

Notice of the Bognor Local Board of Health's proposal to purchase the now dilapidated Jubilee School building as a site for a new Town Hall, first appeared in the local press in June 1880. Protests by residents led to the plans being amended; the existing building was used instead and opened as the Local Board's offices in March 1882. This sufficed until the 1920s when a purpose-built town hall was planned for Clarence Road. The former school building was demolished in 1927 and along with a property on either side, replaced seven years later by the Southdown bus station.

Today, the only reminder of the Jubilee School is a tablet set above the door of the old Church School in Bersted Street. The Latin inscription records that the building, a 'cradle of Christian faith', was rebuilt in 1884 in memory of Charlotte, daughter of the

English King, George IV, and in memory of Queen Victoria's (youngest) son, Leopold, Duke of Albany. This Leopold (not to be confused with Charlotte's husband) was the Prince Consort, who died aged 31 years in March 1884. During a short life marred by ill-health, he had championed the cause of education. Charlotte, of course, was commemorated because some of the money from the recently closed Jubilee School, which she had helped to establish in 1809, had gone to Bersted School.

Jubilee School commemorative plaque, discovered 1927

Sources:

PRO: ED.49/7678, ED.49/7679 (latter includes Jubilee Annual Reort 1824)
Gerard Young Collection, W.S.R.O.: Notes in GY 5001
    and Annual Report 1869
WSRO: E24/9/5. E24/19/8. Par. 19/25/2 (Annual Reports, 1861 & 1863)
Bognor Observer, 23 November 1927.
Sussex Weekly Advertiser, 5 Nov. 1810: Hampshire Telegraph & Sussex
    Chronicle, 8 Sep. 1817.
West Sussex Gazette, 23 Aug. 1860, 14 & 21 Dec. 1865, 19 Sept. 1867
    29 Dec. 1870, 23 July, 1874, 10 July 1879.

N.B. Ron Iden's *Unwillingly to School* - the history of South Bersted Church School in the 19th Century, (1997) is on sale at Bognor Regis Museum, 69, High Street, or from the author at 10a, Devonshire Road.

"Commerce"

THE POLLY ANNE RESTAURANT

(Newsletter No. 2, January 1980)

To most readers of our first newsletter the cover illustration recalled an attractive little corner of Bognor's High Street. Some, however, were mystified and wanted to know where the building stood. So here are some lines about "Polly Anne".

No. 74 High Street stood two doors west of the Bus Station (which is really Nos.66 to 70); roughly opposite Lennox Street. Built soon after the Battle of Trafalgar, it was the end house of Bedford Row, or Bedford Place, a row of houses along the north side of the street as far as London Road (then a cul-de-sac called Dorset Gardens). All had long gardens in front, prompting one guide-book publisher in 1914 to describe High Street as "one of the prettiest in the Kingdom". Today, Torbay Fisheries is a remnant of this row; gardens and houses disappeared one by one after the building line was brought forward in the 1930s.

Various private residents lived here including the Rev. David Price in the 1850s. At the turn of the century the house had been re-named "Talland House" with a Mr. Arthur Pinder in residence in 1905.

Soon after 1910, commerce moved in with Mrs. Susannah Shaw, dealer in second-hand furniture and bric-a-brac. In 1915 a Mr. James Poulett appeared, hiring out bicycles and bath chairs from the forecourt. The garden had been paved over by now, although a piece of it was later reinstated.

Mr. Poulett moved his business to the opposite end of the High Street (no. 9) and in the 1920s "Gray, Misses, Woollen and Knitted Goods" had taken over and in about 1936, converted the ground floor into a cafe which remained as a cozy rendezvous for the next thirty years.

In 1955, this corner was altered beyond recognition, when "progress" next door replaced the Merchant Taylors' Convalescent Home, trees and flint wall with Queensway, and the stark facade of 'Pricerite' Supermarket edged its way into High Street as far as the entrance to its front flats, Gordon House. Not content with this intrusion, the developers purchased Polly Anne's and the next house, demolished them in 1963 and extended the supermarket to the Bus Station.

Apart from the appealing bow-front and the warm pink glow of the interior lighting, the feature I miss most is, in words of the late Gerard Young, "something which distinguished Bognor from other seaside resorts - it had hollyhocks growing in its High Street". One was also made to feel welcome. Nowadays, you're lucky if "Thank you, please call again" is stamped on your checkout receipt.

[N.B. 2004. Torbay Fisheries, at No. 56 High Street, disappeared in the 1980s. (now part of 'Quality Seconds'.) The Bus Station was demolished in 1993.]

MR. HERRINGTON'S FORGE
at SOUTH BERSTED
(Newsletter No. 38, February 1998)

One of my earliest memories is that of watching, spellbound, the shoeing of a carthorse at Herrington's forge on my way home from South Bersted School in the 1950s. I wondered how the noble animal remained so calm while the 'cruel' man placed what seemed to be a red-hot horse-shoe on its hoof and drove the nails home - was it anaesthetized? What I didn't appreciate at the time, of course, was that I was witnessing one of the last vestiges of rural life at Bersted.

The Herrington family first arrived here at the turn of the century. Walter Henry Herrington was born at Slindon in 1857 and married Matilda Hotston, daughter of the landlord of the 'Spur' inn. For 22 years he worked as head blacksmith for Mr. C J

Fletcher on the Dale Park Estate at Madehurst, where his four sons and four daughters were born. Around 1899 Walter and Matilda movd their large family, briefly to Felpham, and then to South Bersted. The forge, at the Chichester Road end of Bersted Street, had already existed for some years, converted by a Mr. Baley from a stonemason's yard. It was eventually bought by a Mr. Wakeland, who sold it to Mr. Herrington.

In 1946, Mr George Baley, of Esmond House in The Steyne, claimed oxen had been shod there 50 years previously. His father had described them as 'local' oxen and "a terrible nuisance" as they had to be 'tied and thrown' (the practice of tying the legs and 'throwing' or laying the animal on its side for shoeing, while the ox-man or boy sat on its neck and held the horns)*.

Bersted Street with Mr Herrington's Forge on the right.

Fields still separated the village of South Bersted from Bognor in 1900 and horses played a major role in the mobility and farming life of the parish, so work was plentiful. Walter died in November 1934, but in 1945, his son, Thomas, who carried on the business, described working from 3 o'clock on a summer's morning till 8 in the evening, fitting 21 cart tyres before breakfast on one occasion. During Goodwood Week early in the century, "shays", carriages and pairs, landaus, brakes, pony traps and four-in-hands used to come along this road and turn off at the Nelson Arms" (at Colworth). Race horses were often shod: they belonged to George Edwardes (of theatrical fame, died 1915) visiting friends nearby, or were housed in horse boxes in Town Cross Avenue or at what was known as 'The Dog Kennel' where shops now face Hawthorn Road, Thomas recalled.

"We couldn't keep pace with demand in the war" he added (referring to 1914-18) and at one time 40 or 50 horses were waiting in the yard and outside, for "branding". "Even today (1945), farmers realise that horses can go where a tractor cannot". Apart from a blacksmith at Pagham, they were the only one along the Bognor to Chichester Road and Mr Herrington, a master farrier responsible for shoeing 72 horses for various customers, still often worked from 6 a.m. to 8 p.m. The firm were now also agricultural engineers and wheelwrights, and his sons undertook acetylene welding.

By the early 1960s the blacksmith side was used more by riding schools than by farmers; cars were now the main means of transport and the firm had adapted accordingly, replacing the old open shed with the modern building that stands today. The farrier's work finished in the early 1980s and the premises now house a car workshop.

Sources:

Bognor Regis Post, 21st July 1945
Bognor Regis Observer 22nd March 1947, 22nd June 1962
Gerard Young Collection at W.S.R.O.
   File GY 5010, page 7/E.1

* N.B. Sussex Red oxen and their crossbreds were reared and used on the Downs for centuries, but an agricultural writer in 1946 could find no record of them being bred near Bognor in the 1890s, although they may have been bought by a local farmer, or were possibly the Welsh black runts, which were then replacing the Sussex as draught cattle. Oxen were more suited than horses to downland slopes and light soil; they were docile and longer working, needing no grooming and only hay and straw for food. But eventually they proved unwieldy for the self-binding reaper and too slow for the quickening pace of life after the first World War. One of the last surviving ox-teams was that of Mr Gorringe, at Exceat Farm, East Sussex, in the late 1920s. For anyone interested, articles and correspondence on the subject appear in the excellent *Sussex County Magazine,* vols 1 (1927), pages 462, 572; vol.4 p.1062; vol.8 p.80; vol.13 p.19; vol.14 p.264; vol.25 (1951) p.49; on local reference library shelves.

SWEET MEMORIES

(Newsletter No. 38, February 1998)

Next door to Herrington's forge at South Bersted stood another port-of-call in my early school days, the confectioners run by the same family. Local street directories list this as a general store run by Mrs Emily Earwicker until Mrs Herrington took over in 1915. (Around the corner, facing Town Cross Avenue, were Nos. 1 and 2 Hamburg Cottages, where Mr W H Wood later opened his cycle shop, now the Chinese Take-away). By 1940 the general store was described as a confectioner's, although in recent years it expanded its floor space and resumed its earlier role, until competition from nearby out-of-town supermarkets led to closure in August 1996. The premises are currently undergoing conversion work.

Back in the 1950s it was still a sweet-shop of the old-fashioned variety. On the pavement outside, my brother and I would press our noses against the window-pane and survey the glass jars filled with wine gums, liquorice allsorts, sherbert lemons, bon-bons coated with icing sugar, aniseed balls which changed colour as you sucked them, multi-shaped broken slabs of peanut brittle, dolly mixtures, pea-sized Tom Thumb drops, fruit pastilles, chocolate limes, chocolate or blackcurrant eclairs, all manner of boiled sweets, and old-fashioned humbugs, which stuck together and had to be prised out of the jar with a spoon or some such metal implement.

But the real centre of attraction was the shelf below, whereon sat the trays containing a veritable array of smaller items more suited to those with limited pocket-money. Here were (pre-decimalisation) penny chews, halfpenny chews, farthing chews, or even 8-a-penny chews; little chewy squares wrapped in black and white check paper ('black jacks') or red and yellow (nicknamed 'rhubarb and custard' - tasting of raspberry and banana?)

Then there were sherbert fountains (how we choked on the sherbert when we sucked on the liquorice straws!); circular pastel-shaded 'flying saucers' filled with the hazardous sherbert; cheap chocolate coated with rice paper (tasted foul!); sweet cigarettes of dolly mixture texture, white with red tips (sold in orange paper packets or loose); liquorice pipes and bootlaces, liquorice strips wound in circles with a liquorice allsort at the centre; yellow coloured liquorice roots; 'jamboree packs' containing a free gift (a metal clicker, or plastic car?); and a vague memory of brown, fibrous coconutty items..

The list is endless! Pineapply cubes, cola cubes, gob-stoppers large and small, palma violets, love-hearts bearing messages, refreshers, spangles, packs of 'imps' (tiny match-heads which burnt the tongue), bars of coconut ice or honeycomb, palm toffee (toffee on the outside with banana and strawberry flavoured strips in the middle) or toffee slabs which had to be broken with a hammer, and of course, bars of chocolate - Peter's (dark) chocolate, Fry's (gooey centred) chocolate cream and the famous Fry's '5 boys' - thin chocolate bars imprinted wth the faces of five boys each sporting a different expression (see photograph at end of article).

Inside the wooden-floored shop (much smaller in those days), stood a kindly lady (was she Mrs Herrington?) behind a tiny counter bearing more trays of goodies and surrounded by more glass jars. She would patiently await our decision before removing one of those heavy jars from the shelf; I recall the clatter of loose sweets tipped into the metal scales for weighing, the rustle of paper bags which received our humble purchases - a quarter for 6d or 2 ounces for 3d - and the 'ching-ching' of the old style till as she received our loose pence!

Today, Woolworth's pick and mix and the self-selection at some open-all-hours stores offer similar facilities, but with copious Euro-regulated hygienic wrappings and the ubiquitous plastic bag, and lacking surely the variety and personal service we experienced at the little sweet shop of fond memory at South Bersted. Ah! the magic of nostalgia!

FRY'S MILK CHOCOLATE

DESPERATION. PACIFICATION. EXPECTATION. ACCLAMATION. REALIZATION.
ITS FRY'S

J.S. FRY & SONS L.ᵗᵈ BRISTOL & LONDON.

(Can any reader add to the list of sweets, compiled during a recent conversation with Paul and Irene Sangster? Irene also remembers having the back wheels of her broken doll's pushchair repaired at the blacksmith's!)

FAREWELL TO 'LONG & STRICKLAND.'

(Newsletter No.42 February 2000)

On a medical theme, the new century has begun in traditional style in Bognor Regis with the demise of Springfield House (the original War Memorial Hospital in Chichester Road), and the closure of another local institution - the chemist shop at no. 21 High Street, which has served generations of Bognorians for the past 147 years - 138 of them under the name of Mr Long. or Long and Strickland.

Nos. 21 to 25 High Street were built on meadowland as one unit sometime in the mid to late 1840s and were first known as 1, 2 & 3 York Terrace (stand across the road and you will see how refurbishment of no. 25 in 1979, for new offices of the Sussex County Building Society -- now Neal Smith estate agents - marred the symmetry of the terrace's facade).

From an advertisement in a 'Homeland' Bognor Guide Book, 1925

Depending on which written source you consult, the firm was established at no.21 (alias 1 York Terrace) in 1853, 1860 or 1862. Evidence from trades directories and census returns suggests that it was Henry James from Kent who first set up business there as a pharmaceutist in 1853, selling up nine years later to Alfred Thorby Long.

Mr .Long was born in Brighton and probably moved to Bognor after his marriage to Mary Ann Catt, at Ringmer, near Lewes, in June 1862. In the 1871 census returns, aged 34, he was living above his High Street shop, with three house-servants and a 25-year-old chemist's assistant named Absalom Whitehouse Strickland. In the mid 1870s, Mr.Long bought himself one of the new houses being erected in Sudley road - Firle Villa at no.19 (now gone) - and took his assistant into partnership, re-naming the business 'Long & Strickland'.

Alfred Thorby Long (W.S.R.O.: UD/BR/65/1/1)

For much of his life in Bognor Mr.Long served as member of the Local Board, he was the first Chairman of its successor, the Urban District Council in 1894-1895, and a County Councillor for nine years. (He had, said his obituary in April 1910, "little sympathy with the modern tendency to Socialism and revolutionary changes") He was a leading light in free-masonry, a churchwarden at St.John's Church for 43 years, director of several local companies, committee member for Graylingwell Hospital and, during any spare time, a keen sportsman. Nevertheless, his funeral service was described as "quite simple, as was befitting the character of Mr Long, whose simple, kindly nature was averse to ostentation of any kind ... he was one of Nature's gentlemen."

Mr. Strickland, who married in 1882, died three months before Mr.Long, at the age of 60. His funeral was a far more impressive military affair, for he was a founder member of the Bognor Company of Volunteers for twenty years, rising from Colour Sergeant to Ambulance Sergeant. He also served as Secretary for the defunct Bognor Literary Society and sidesman at St.Wilfrid's Church.

The business was taken over by Norman R.Hilton, becoming a limited company in the late 'twenties, with branches in Essex Road, in The Broadway near Felpham's Snook Corner, and at Barnham. These were later sold, but the High Street shop continued under courteous Mr.Jack Cooper, who many still fondly recall (he died in 1990). For a few years, 'Long & Strickland' was submerged under the chain names of Aston's, R.J.Dawe and Advantage Chemists, but along with a new shop interior, it was restored in 1988 by director Naeem Abdul, who recognised the trading value of a familiar name.

From the Bognor 'Official Guide'
published by Webster & Webb c.1905

Alongside two old photographs of the shop in the local *Observer* in 1976, a Mr.Fred Holden recalled starting work there on leaving South Bersted School in 1918. 'In those days, a chemist had to mix his own potions and my job was to wash up the bowls, bottles,etc. and keep the shop clean and tidy. Mr and Mrs.Hilton and Miss Reynolds did the harder work.

Sources:- Bognor (Regis) Observer, 26 Jan. 2 Feb. 20 & 27 April 1910; 9 April 1976, Bognor Regis Guardian and Post, 17 Oct. 1990 (beware of dating errors). Wills - WSRO; STM 28 pp 254, 318. Census returns, trades directories, advertisements in Bognor directories and guide-books.